C.L.I.M.B. Through Retirement

A SHERPA'S GUIDE
TO NAVIGATING YOUR JOURNEY

Brad Jones | Jones Retirement Advisors

Copyright © 2024 by Brad Jones and Advisors Excel, LLC.

All rights reserved. No part of this publication may be reproduced, distributed, or transmitted in any form or by any means, including photocopying, recording, or other electronic or mechanical methods, without the prior written permission of the publisher, except in the case of brief quotations embodied in critical reviews and certain other noncommercial uses permitted by copyright law. For permission requests, write to the publisher at the address below. These materials are provided to you by Brad Jones for informational purposes only and Brad Jones and Advisors Excel, LLC expressly disclaim any and all liability arising out of or relating to your use of same. The provision of these materials does not constitute legal or investment advice and does not establish an attorney-client relationship between you and Brad Jones. No tax advice is contained in these materials. You are solely responsible for ensuring the accuracy and completeness of all materials as well as the compliance, validity, and enforceability of all materials under any applicable law. The advice and strategies found within may not be suitable for every situation. You are expressly advised to consult with a qualified attorney or other professional in making any such determination and to determine your legal or financial needs. No warranty of any kind, implied, expressed, or statutory, including but not limited to the warranties of title and non-infringement of third-party rights, is given with respect to this publication.

Brad Jones | Jones Retirement Advisors
230 N. 2nd St., Suite 200
Brighton, MI 48116
jonesretirement.com

Book layout ©2022 Advisors Excel, LLC

C.L.I.M.B. Through Retirement/Brad Jones

ISBN 9798320258003

Brad Jones is registered as an Investment Advisor Representative and is a licensed insurance agent in the state of Michigan. Jones Retirement Advisors is an independent financial services firm that helps individuals create retirement strategies using a variety of investment and insurance products to custom suit their needs and objectives.

Insurance products are offered through the insurance business Jones Retirement Advisors. Jones Retirement Advisors is also an Investment Advisory practice that offers products and services through AE Wealth Management, LLC (AEWM), a Registered Investment Adviser. AEWM does not offer insurance products. The insurance products offered by Jones Retirement Advisors are not subject to Investment Adviser requirements. AEWM and Jones Retirement Advisors are not affiliated companies.

Securities products and services made available through AE Financial Services, LLC (AEFS), member FINRA/SIPC. Investment advisory products and services made available through AE Wealth Management, LLC (AEWM), a Registered Investment Advisor.

The contents of this book are provided for informational purposes only and are not intended to serve as the basis for any financial decisions. Any tax, legal, or estate planning information is general in nature. Please remember that converting an employer plan account to a Roth IRA is a taxable event. Increased taxable income from the Roth IRA conversion may have several consequences. Be sure to consult with a qualified tax advisor before making any decisions regarding your IRA. It should not be construed as legal or tax advice. Always consult an attorney or tax professional regarding the applicability of this information to your unique situation.

Information presented is believed to be factual and up-to-date, but we do not guarantee its accuracy, and it should not be regarded as a complete analysis of the subjects discussed. All expressions of opinion are those of the author as of the date of publication and are subject to change. Content should not be construed as personalized investment advice nor should it be interpreted as an offer to buy or sell any securities mentioned. A financial advisor should be consulted before implementing any of the strategies presented.

Investing involves risk, including the potential loss of principal. No investment strategy can guarantee a profit or protect against loss in periods of declining values. Any references to protection benefits or guaranteed/lifetime income streams refer only to fixed insurance products, not securities or investment products. Insurance and annuity product guarantees are backed by the financial strength and claims-paying ability of the issuing insurance company. Jones Retirement Advisors is not affiliated with the U.S. government or any governmental agency.

Any names used in the examples in this book are hypothetical only and do not represent actual clients.

"The harder I work, the luckier I get."

*~ Samuel Goldwyn,
film producer and founder of Goldwyn Pictures*

Table of Contents

The Importance of Planning i
Longevity 1
Taxes 21
Market Volatility 33
Retirement Income 41
Social Security 57
401(k)s, IRAs, and Roth IRAs 73
Annuities 85
Estate & Legacy 95
Women Retire Too 105
Indexed Universal Life Insurance 117
Finding a Financial Professional 125
Acknowledgments 129
About the Author 131

PREFACE

The Importance of Planning

Retire late or die early. When my father came to me in his mid-fifties and said he wanted to retire by age sixty-five, I told him it wasn't possible and that his only options were to either retire late or die early. Naturally, he was upset by that response, but it was the truth.

Don't misunderstand; I have great parents, and growing up, we had plenty of love to go around. They were not great with money, however. While we weren't tragically poor my entire childhood, we lived what I call paycheck-to-Wednesday, meaning we made it twelve days in a fourteen-day pay cycle before running out of money. Every Wednesday, we would go to Farmer Jack for groceries, and my mother would write a personal check because she knew it wouldn't clear until Friday—payday.

As you might imagine, living paycheck-to-Wednesday caused my parents significant stress. When I think back to their disagreements, most stemmed from the anxiety they felt around their lack of resources. Watching them struggle had a profound impact on me as a young child. I got my first job delivering papers when I was thirteen because I knew if there were things I wanted, I would have to buy them myself—not because my parents didn't want to give me and my siblings the things we wanted, but because they simply couldn't afford to.

Growing up, I knew I didn't want to live paycheck-to-Wednesday. I didn't want to experience the same stress around money my parents had. However, while I knew what I *didn't* want, I wasn't sure what I *did* want by way of a career. I'd always loved math and people. Despite being a quiet kid, I'd always been a jokester, but never in a mean way. One of my friend's parents used to say, "Brad's got to be a bad kid. He's so nice; it has to be fake." Though I was shy, I loved connecting with people. I was naturally smart and willing to work hard for what I wanted. How could I integrate those qualities into a fulfilling career? I had no idea.

I was a junior in high school when I came across a college brochure that gave the average salaries for various careers, including the salary of a financial advisor. I had no idea what a financial advisor was or did, but the salary looked good, so I decided that's what I would be. For the next several years, I put my head down and studied hard. When I was twenty-one, I graduated from Eastern Michigan University with a degree in finance. However, I still didn't really understand what a financial advisor did until I started doing the work myself.

After college, I officially joined the financial services industry. I was living in my parent's basement and working sixty hours a week at a job I had essentially stumbled into—a job that also turned out to be my life's calling. I was finally learning what a financial advisor did. I discovered this job is more than just the numbers and the math; it is about making a real difference in people's lives—people like my parents, who made some missteps, and people who are good with money but still aren't sure if they could ever retire. One of my greatest joys is developing a financial plan for someone and seeing the look of joy and relief on their face once they realize they're going to be okay and have options beyond retiring late or dying early.

I've been a financial advisor for nearly two decades, and I've helped people from all walks of life and almost every financial situation you can imagine. If you take nothing else away from this book, I hope you take this to heart: *the importance of a comprehensive financial plan cannot be overstated.*

You might be thinking, "I've got $2 million (or whatever amount) in savings. I'm good."

Here's the second biggest thing I want you to understand: *Having X amount in savings is not the same as having a plan.* Sometimes, it's not even as good as having a plan. Allow me to explain.

Let's say we have a couple, Robert and Sue. During their working years, they're diligent with their savings and live a frugal lifestyle. A few years into their retirement, Robert suddenly passes away. He was the one who handled all the finances, but their son is a financial planner. Naturally, Sue turns to him for advice. She has only one question: Am I going to be okay?

After reviewing their accounts, Sue's son has good news: Sue and Robert had managed to save several million dollars. She is going to be just fine! Hearing this, Sue begins to cry, but not because she's happy.

"What's wrong?" her son asks. "You have plenty of money; you'll be okay."

"That's not why I'm upset," Sue replies. "I had no idea we had so much. Your dad and I could have done so much more while he was still here."

I see situations just like this all the time. Without a proper plan, even people who'd built a decent nest egg become scared to spend money. As a result, they miss out on a lot of things they could have done. Maybe they didn't need to work those extra years just to get to X amount in savings; perhaps they didn't need that much. They could have enjoyed a few more years of retirement, vacations, or special times with their families and loved ones.

Obviously, saving is important, but a plan can give you the structure to know how much you really need. Depending on your goals and desired lifestyle, that amount might not be as much as you think. And if you haven't saved enough, a structured plan can help you set realistic goals to get you where you need to be. A proper plan helps eliminate the retire late or die early options.

Let's revisit my parents for a moment. As I've noted, they struggled a lot financially, which caused them a great deal of stress and tension. They ended up losing the house I grew up in, mainly due to their inability to manage their resources. It was a stressful time.

My parents wanted to retire by the time they were in their mid-sixties. I was serious when I told my dad this plan wasn't possible—not unless they made some big changes.

"What do you mean?" my dad asked.

"Are you willing to quit smoking cigarettes?"

He immediately said yes, but here's the thing: My dad had been smoking since he was ten years old. He said "yes" the way most of us say yes to losing weight—by saying we'll start tomorrow. This is also how many people approach saving for retirement: putting it off until the fabled "someday" when they have more time, more energy, more . . . something. This was the approach my parents took.

Despite some serious challenges, my parents' story is one of my greatest successes. I'll reveal more about their situation later in the book. For now, let's get into why you likely cracked the cover of this book in the first place: You're looking for solid, unbiased financial information that will help you gain financial independence and confidently enter your retirement years. My goal is to help you do just that.

Let's get started.

Potential Risks to Your Ideal Retirement

Ever feel like life gets in the way and prevents you from doing things you shouldn't ignore? I think if we're honest with ourselves, we've all put off obligations we know are important. In your case, you may be reading this book because it's time to get serious about financial planning and, specifically, devising a way to ideally prepare for retirement. A retirement plan should be based on more components than just your investments or your finances. The preparation of that strategy begins with your desires, ambitions, and goals for this fulfilling season of life.

There's no such thing as a silly question — not when one of the most common questions we hear from folks regarding retirement is, "Am I going to be okay?" It often seems people are reluctant to meet with financial professionals because they worry they might sound uneducated. However, it's understandable for you to be a novice when it comes to financial issues and retirement concerns. You've been busy with your lives and your careers. Time spent away from work has meant time spent being around those you love and engaging in the activities you enjoy. Retirement provides the opportunity to do even more of that, while not fretting over work obligations.

Concerns people have about what they may encounter during retirement can be far-reaching and still perfectly legitimate. For a quick snapshot, I want to provide a brief sampling of wide-ranging issues that can come up during discussions about what to potentially brace for in retirement. This book will touch on many of these issues in further detail.

Politics: A presidential election often stirs emotions regarding potential effects on the economy. Investors grow anxious about how a new president can influence market returns. It's Congress, however, that establishes tax laws and passes spending bills. Yet the president can indirectly affect the economy and the stock market in various ways such as the appointment of policymakers, development of international relations, and influential sway on new legislation.

Taxes: An example of a president's influence can be cited in signature legislation passed during Donald Trump's presidency, the Tax Cuts and Jobs Act of 2017. However, our tax system remains progressive, so the more you earn, the higher the tax rate within each tax bracket of subsequently higher income. A thorough understanding of tax regulations can be crucial. A financial professional can help identify potential issues a tax professional can help solve.

Inflation: General increases in the prices of goods and services, often measured using the consumer price index (CPI) often stem from fluctuations in real demand for goods and services. Inflation can discourage investment, as well as shortages in goods. A retiree's income can be impacted by the effect inflation can have on a fixed budget. The value of currency decreases because inflation erodes purchasing power.

Cybersecurity: Think you'll give up your smartphone in retirement? No way, right? It's here to stay, along with other intellectual gadgetry, including devices that have not been patented or invented yet. Retirees are becoming more tech-savvy, yet they can also be more trusting, which can be problematic when responding to potential scammers by phone, text, or email. Cybercrime often uses technology to target potential victims. Scammers, much like technology, figure to only grow more sophisticated over time.

CHAPTER 1

Longevity

You would think the prospect of the grave would loom more frightening as we age, yet many retirees say their number one concern is actually running out of money in their twilight years.[1] Unfortunately, this concern is justified because of one significant factor: We're living longer.

According to the Social Security Administration's 2011 Trustee Report, in 1950, the average life expectancy for a sixty-five-year-old man was seventy-eight, and the average for a sixty-five-year-old woman was eighty-one.[2] In the 2023 Trustees Report issued by the SSA, those averages were eighty-three and eighty-six, respectively.[3]

The bottom line of many retirees' budget woes comes down to this: They just didn't plan to live so long. Now, when we are younger and in our working years, that's not something we necessarily see as a bad thing; don't some people fantasize about living forever or, at least, reaching the ripe old age of 100?

---

[1] Brett Arends. MarketWatch. June 5, 2023. "Americans are 'more afraid of running out of money than death.'
https://www.marketwatch.com/story/americans-are-more-afraid-of-running-out-money-than-death-ee5e22e9t
[2] ssa.gov. "Actuarial Publications: Cohort Life Expectancy"
https://www.ssa.gov/oact/TR/2011/lr5a4.html
[3] Kay Dee Cole. claritywealthdevelopment.com. July 6, 2022. "What is the Average Life Expectancy for a 65-year-old?"
https://claritywealthdevelopment.com/blog/what-is-the-average-life-expectancy-for-a-65-year-old

However, with a longer lifespan, we face a few snags as we retire. Our resources are finite — we only have so much money to provide income — but our lifespans can be unpredictably long, perhaps longer than our resources allow. Also, longer lives don't necessarily equate with healthier lives. The longer you live, the more money you will likely need to spend on health care, even excluding long-term care needs like nursing homes.

You will also run into inflation. If you don't plan to live another twenty-five years but end up doing so, inflation at an average of 3 percent will approximately double the price of goods over that time period. To put a harsh twist on that, the buying power of a ninety-year-old will be half of what they would have possessed if they had retired at sixty-five.[4]

Because we don't necessarily get to have our cake and eat it, too, our collective increased longevity hasn't necessarily increased the healthy years of our lives. Typically, our life-extending care most widely applies to the time in our lives when we will need more care in general. Think of common situations like a pacemaker at eighty-five, or cancer treatment at seventy-eight.

"Wow, Brad," I can hear you say. "Way to start with the good news first."

I know, I've painted a grim picture, but all I'm concerned about here is cost. It's hard to put a dollar sign on life, but that is essentially what we're talking about when discussing longevity and finances. Living longer isn't a bad thing; it just costs more, and one key to a sound retirement strategy is preparing for it in advance.

Here's a story of one woman that illustrates this picture perfectly. Her mother passed away in her late seventies after years of suffering from Alzheimer's disease. Her father died at eighty from cancer. With modern medicine and treatment, this woman survived two rounds of breast cancer, lived with

---

[4] Bob Sullivan, Benjamin Curry. Forbes. April 28, 2021. "Inflation And Retirement Investments: What You Need to Know"
https://www.forbes.com/advisor/retirement/inflation-retirement-investments/

diabetes, and relied on a pacemaker, extending her life to age eighty-eight — nearly a decade beyond what she anticipated. However, she and her husband had saved and planned for "just in case," trying to be prepared if they had to move, needed nursing home care, or needed to help children and grandchildren with their expenses.

One of their "just-in-case" scenarios was living much longer than they anticipated. The last six years of her life were fraught with medical expenses, but she was also blessed with knowing her five great-grandchildren and deepening relationships with her children and grandchildren. She was able to pay for her own medical care, including her final two years in a nursing home, and her twilight years were truly golden.

From age eighty-five to eighty-eight, she was more socially active, with many visits from family and friends. She participated in more activities than she had in the seven years since her husband died. Her planning from decades earlier allowed her to pass on a legacy to her children when she passed away herself. The legacy she left behind can be measured both in dollar signs *and* in other intangible ways.[*]

Living longer may be more expensive, but it can be so meaningful when you plan for your "just-in-cases."

Retiring Early

A key part of planning for retirement revolves around retirement income. After all, retirement is cutting the cord that tethers you to your employer — and your monthly check. However, that check often comes with many other benefits, particularly health care. Health care is often the thing that can unexpectedly put dreams for an early retirement on hold. Some employers offer health benefits to their retired workers, but

---

[*] This is a hypothetical example provided for illustrative purposes only; it does not represent a real life scenario, and should not be construed as advice designed to meet the particular needs of an individual's situation.

that number has declined drastically over the past several decades.

In 1988, among employers who offered health benefits to their workers, 66 percent offered health benefits to their retirees. That number has since dwindled to 21 percent[5] So, with employer-offered retirement health benefits on the wane, this becomes a major point of concern for anyone who is looking to retire, particularly those who are looking to retire before age sixty-five, when they would become eligible for Medicare coverage.

Fidelity estimates that the average retired couple at age sixty-five will need approximately $315,000 for health care expenses in retirement, not including long-term care.[6] Do you think it's likely that cost will decrease?

Even if you are working until age sixty-five or have plans to cover your health expenses until that point, I often have clients who incorrectly assume Medicare is their golden ticket to cover all expenses. That is simply not the case.

Retiring Later

Planning for a long life in retirement partly depends on when you retire. While many people end up retiring earlier than they anticipated — due to injuries, layoffs, family crises, and other unforeseen circumstances — continuing to work past age sixty (and even sixty-five) is still a viable option for others and can be an excellent way to help establish financial confidence in retirement.

There are many reasons for this. For one, you obviously still earn a paycheck and the benefits accompanying it. Medical

---

[5] Henry J. Kaiser Family Foundation. October 27, 2022. "2022 Employer Health Benefits Survey Section Eleven: Retiree Health Benefits" https://www.kff.org/report-section/ehbs-2022-section-11-retiree-health-benefits/

[6] Fidelity Viewpoints. Fidelity. August 29, 2022. "How to Plan for Rising Health Care Costs" https://www.fidelity.com/viewpoints/personal-finance/plan-for-rising-health-care-costs

coverage and beefing up your retirement accounts with further savings can be significant by themselves, but continuing to generate income should also keep you from dipping into your retirement funds, further allowing them the opportunity to grow.

Additionally, for many workers, their nine-to-five job is more than just clocking in and out. Having a sense of purpose can keep us active physically, mentally, and socially. That kind of activity and level of engagement may also help stave off many of the health problems that plague retirees. Avoiding a sedentary life is one of the advantages of staying plugged into the workforce, if possible.

Let's look at another example. A man we'll call Henry is an auctioneer for a well-known company. He loves his work, and even though he's nearing retirement age, he has no plans to quit working. As fate would have it, right around the time Henry could have retired, the company he works for decides to shake things up internally.

All the company's auctioneers—including Henry—are now classified as independent contractors, meaning they can work as much or as little as they like. This works out for Henry, who decides to retire partially. He works two or three days a week at a job he loves and spends the other days on the golf course. He continues to provide a great life for his family while enjoying more freedom with his schedule. Best of all? He's maintaining an active, purpose-filled life even in semi-retirement. We should all be as lucky as Henry.*

Health Care

Take a second to reflect on your health care plan. Although working up to or even past age sixty-five could allow you to avoid a coverage gap between your working years and

---

* This is a hypothetical example provided for illustrative purposes only; it does not represent a real life scenario, and should not be construed as advice designed to meet the particular needs of an individual's situation.

Medicare, that may not be an option for you. Even if it is, when you retire, you will need to make some decisions about what kind of insurance coverage you may need to supplement your Medicare. Are there any medical needs you have that may require coverage in addition to Medicare? Did your parents or grandparents have any inherited medical conditions you might consider using a special savings plan to cover?

These are all questions that are important to review with your financial professional so you can be sure you have enough money put aside for health care.

Long-Term Care

Longevity means the need for long-term care is statistically more likely to happen. If you intend to pass on a legacy, planning for long-term care is paramount, since most estimates project nearly 70 percent of Americans who reach age sixty-five will need some type of it.[7] However, this may be one of the biggest, most stressful pieces of longevity planning I encounter in my work. For one thing, who wants to talk about the point in their lives when they may feel the most limited? Who wants to dwell on what will happen if they can no longer toilet, bathe, dress, or feed themselves?

I get it; this is a less-than-fun part of planning. But a little bit of preparation now can go a long way!

When it comes to your longevity, just like with your goals, one of the important things to do is sit and dream. It may not be the fun, road-trip-to-the-Grand-Canyon kind of dreaming, but you can spend time envisioning how you want your twilight years to look.

For instance, if it is important for you to live in your home for as long as possible, who will provide for the day-to-day fixes

---

[7] Claire Samuels. aPlaceforMom.com. September 13, 2023. "Long-Term Care Statistics: A Portrait of Americans in Assisted Living, Nursing Homes, and Skilled Nursing Facilities" https://www.aplaceformom.com/senior-living-data/articles/long-term-care-statistics

and to-dos of housework if you become ill? Will you set aside money for a service, or do you have relatives or friends nearby whom you could comfortably allow to help you? Do you prefer in-home care over a nursing home or assisted living? This could be a good time to discuss the possibility of moving into a retirement community versus staying where you are or whether it's worth moving to another state and leaving relatives behind.

These are all important factors to discuss with your spouse and children, as *now* is the right time to address questions and concerns. For instance, is aging in place more important to one spouse than the other? Are the friends or relatives who live nearby emotionally, physically, and financially capable of helping you for a time if you face an illness?

Many families I meet with find these conversations very uncomfortable, particularly when children discuss nursing home care with their parents. A knee-jerk reaction for many is to promise they will care for their aging parents. This is noble and well-intentioned, but there needs to be an element of realism here. Does "help" from an adult child mean they stop by and help you with laundry, cooking, home maintenance, and bills? Or does it mean they move you into their spare room when you have hip surgery? Are they prepared to help you use the restroom and bathe if that becomes difficult for you to do on your own?

I don't mean to discourage families from caring for their own; this can be a profoundly admirable relationship when it works out. However, I've seen families put off planning for late-in-life care based on a tenuous promise that the adult children would care for their parents, only to watch as the support system crumbles. Sometimes, this is because the assumed caregiver hasn't given serious thought to the preparation they would need, both in a formal sense and regarding their personal physical, emotional, and financial commitments. This is often also because we can't see the future: Alzheimer's disease and other maladies of old age can exact a heavy toll. When a loved one reaches the point where they are at risk of wandering away or need help with two or more activities of daily living, it can be more than one person or a family can realistically handle.

If you know what you want, communicate with your family about both the best-case and worst-case scenarios. Then, hope for the best, and plan for the worst.

Realistic Cost of Care

Included in your planning should be a consideration for the cost of long-term care. The potential costs for such care and treatment can be underestimated, especially by those who have maintained robust health and find it difficult to envision future declines in their condition.

Another piece of planning for long-term care costs is anticipating inflation. It's common knowledge that prices have been and keep rising, which can lower your purchasing power on everything from food to medical care. Long-term care is a big piece of the inflation-disparity pie.

While local costs vary from state to state, the following table shows the national median for various forms of long-term care (plus projections that account for a 3 percent annual inflation, so you can see what I am referencing):[8]

---

[8] Nationwide. 2022. "Compare Long-term Care costs from state to state" https://nationwidefinancialltcmap.hvsfinancial.com/

Long-Term Care Costs: Inflation				
	Informal Care	Home Care	Assisted Living	Nursing Home (semi-private room)
Annual 2024	$42,037	$33,621	$60,874	$113,522
Annual 2034	$56,495	$45,184	$81,810	$160,134
Annual 2044	$75,924	$60,723	$109,945	$225,884
Annual 2054	$102,036	$81,607	$147,757	$318,632

Fund Your Long-Term Care

One common mistake I see occurs in those who haven't planned for long-term care because they assume the government will provide everything. But that's a big misconception. The government has two health insurance programs: Medicare and Medicaid. These can greatly assist you in your health care *needs* in retirement but usually don't provide enough coverage to cover all your health care *costs* in retirement. My firm isn't a government outpost, so we don't get to make decisions regarding policy and specifics about either of these programs. I'm going to give an overview of both, but if you want to dive into the details of these programs, you can visit www.Medicare.gov and www.Medicaid.gov.

Medicare
Medicare covers those aged sixty-five and older and those who are disabled. Medicare's coverage of any nursing-home-related health issues is limited. It might cover your nursing home stay

if it is not a "custodial" stay and isn't long-term. For example, if you break a bone or suffer a stroke, stay in a nursing home for rehabilitative care, and then return home, Medicare may cover you. However, if you have developed dementia or are looking to move to a nursing facility because you can no longer bathe, dress, toilet, feed yourself, or take care of your hygiene, etc., then Medicare is not going to pay for your nursing home costs.[9]

You can enroll in Medicare anytime during the three months before and three months after your sixty-fifth birthday. Miss your enrollment deadline, and you could risk paying increased premiums for the rest of your life.[10] On top of prompt enrollment, there are a few other things to think about when it comes to Medicare, not least among them being the need to understand the different "parts," what they do, and what they don't cover.

Part A

Medicare Part A is what you might think of as "classic" Medicare. Hospital care, some types of home health care, and major medical care fall under this. While most enrollees pay nothing for this service (as they likely paid into the system for at least ten years), you might have to, based on either work history or delayed signup. In 2024, the highest premium is $505 per month, and a hospital stay does have a deductible — $1,632.[11] Also, if you have a hospital stay that surpasses sixty days, you could be looking at additional costs; keep in mind, Medicare doesn't pay for long-term care and services.

---

[9] Medicare.gov. "What Part A covers" https://www.medicare.gov/what-medicare-covers/part-a/what-part-a-covers.html
[10] Medicare.gov. "When can I sign up for Medicare?" https://www.medicare.gov/basics/get-started-with-medicare/sign-up/when-can-i-sign-up-for-medicare
[11] CMS.gov. October 12, 2023. "2024 Medicare Parts A & B Premiums and Deductibles" https://www.cms.gov/newsroom/fact-sheets/2024-medicare-parts-b-premiums-and-deductibles?ref=biztoc.com

Part B

Medicare Part B is an essential piece of wrap-around coverage for Medicare Part A. It helps pay for doctor visits and outpatient services. This also comes with a price tag: Although the Part B annual deductible is only $240 in 2024, you will still pay 20 percent of all costs after that, with no limit on out-of-pocket expenses. The Part B monthly premium for 2024 ranges from the standard amount of $174.70 to $594.[12]

Part C

Medicare Part C (more commonly known as a Medicare Advantage plan) is an alternative to a combination of Parts A, B, and sometimes D. Administered through private insurance companies, these have a variety of costs and restrictions, and they are subject to the specific policies and rules of the issuing carrier.

Part D

Medicare Part D is also offered through a private insurer and is supplemental to Parts A and B, as its primary purpose is to cover prescription drugs. Like any private insurance plan, Part D has its quirks and rules that vary from insurer to insurer.

The Donut Hole
Even with a "Part D" in place, you may still have a coverage gap between what your Part D private drug insurance pays for your prescription and what basic Medicare pays. In 2024, the coverage gap is $5,030, meaning that after you meet your private prescription insurance limit, you will spend no more

---

[12] Ibid.

than 25 percent of your drug costs out-of-pocket before Medicare kicks in to pay for more prescription drugs.[13]

Note: In the donut hole, you pay up to 25 percent out of pocket for all covered medications. You leave the donut hole once you've spent $8,000 out of pocket for covered drugs in 2024. 2024 is the last year for the donut hole. A $2,000 out-of-pocket cap takes effect for Medicare Part D in 2025.

Medicare Supplements

Medicare Supplement Insurance, MedSupp, Medigap, or plans labeled Medicare Part F, G, H, I, J ... Known by a variety of monikers, this is just a fancy way of saying "medical coverage for those over sixty-five that picks up the tab for whatever the federal Medicare program(s) doesn't." Again, costs, limitations, etc., vary by carrier.

Does that sound like a bunch of government alphabet soup to you? It certainly does to me. And did you read the fine print? Unpredictable costs, varied restrictions, difficult-to-compare benefits, donut holes, and coverage gaps. That's par for the course with health care plans throughout our adult lives. What gives? I thought Medicare was supposed to be easier, comprehensive, and at no cost!

The truth is there is probably no stage of life when health care is easy to understand.

The best thing you can do for yourself is to scope out the health care field early, compare costs often, and prepare for out-of-pocket costs well in advance — decades, if possible.

Medicaid

Medicaid is a program the states administer, so funding, protocol, and limitations vary. Compared to Medicare,

---

[13] Medicare. "Costs in the coverage gap" https://www.medicare.gov/drug-coverage-part-d/costs-for-medicare-drug-coverage/costs-in-the-coverage-gap

Medicaid more widely covers nursing home care, but it targets a different demographic: those with low incomes.

If you have more assets than the Medicaid limit in your state and need nursing home care, you will need to use those assets to pay for your care. You will also have a list of additional state-approved ways to use or spend some of these assets over the Medicaid limit, such as pre-purchasing burial plots and funeral expenses or paying off debts. After that, your remaining assets fund your nursing home stay until they are gone, at which point Medicaid will jump in.

Some people aren't stymied by this, thinking they will just pass on their financial assets early by gifting them to relatives, friends, and causes so they can qualify for Medicaid when they need it. However, to prevent this exact scenario, Uncle Sam has implemented what's called the "look-back period." Currently, if you enroll in Medicaid, you are subject to having the government scrutinize the last five years of your finances for large gifts or expenses that may subject you to penalties, temporarily making you ineligible for Medicaid coverage.

So, if you're planning to preserve your money for future generations and retain control of your financial resources during your lifetime, you'll probably want to prepare for the costs of longevity beyond a "government plan."

Self-Funding

One way to fund a longer life is the old-fashioned way, through self-funding. There are a variety of financial tools you can use, and they all have their pros and cons. If your assets are in low-interest financial vehicles (savings, bonds, CDs), you risk letting inflation erode the value of your dollar. If you are relying on the stock market, you have more growth potential, but you'll also want to consider the possible implications of market volatility. What if your assets take a hit? If you suffer a loss in your retirement portfolio in early or mid-retirement, you might have the option to "tighten your belt," so to speak, and cut back on discretionary spending to allow your portfolio the room to bounce back. But if you are retired and depend on income from a stock account that just hit a downward stride, what are you going to do?

HSAs

These days, you might also be able to self-fund through a health savings account (HSA) if you have access to one through a high-deductible health plan (you will not qualify to save in an HSA after enrolling in Medicare). In an HSA, any growth of your tax-deductible contributions will be tax-free, and any distributions paid out for qualified health costs are also tax-free. Long-term care expenses count as health costs, so if this is an option available to you, it is one way to use the tax advantages to self-fund your longevity. Bear in mind if you are younger than sixty-five, any money you use for non-qualified expenses will be subject to taxes and penalties, and if you are older than sixty-five, any HSA money you use for non-medical expenses is subject to income tax.

LTCI

One slightly more nuanced way to pay for longevity — specifically for long-term care — is long-term care insurance (LTCI). As car insurance protects your assets in case of a car accident and home insurance protects your assets in case something happens to your house, long-term care insurance aims to help protect your assets in case you need long-term care in an at-home or nursing home situation.

As with other types of insurance, you will pay a monthly or annual premium in exchange for an insurance company paying for long-term care down the road. Typically, policies cover two to three years of care, which is adequate for an "average" situation: it's estimated that 70 percent of Americans aged sixty-five and older will need long-term care of some kind.[14]

---

[14] Claire Samuels. aplaceformom.com. September 13, 2023. "Portrait of Americans in Assisted Living, Nursing Homes, and Skilled Nursing Facilities" https://www.aplaceformom.com/senior-living-data/articles/long-term-care-statistics

Now, there are a few oft-cited components of LTCI that make it unattractive for some:

- Expense — LTCI can be expensive. It is generally less expensive the younger you are, but a sixty-five-year-old couple who purchased LTCI in 2023 could expect to pay a combined annual amount of $3,750 for a policy. And the annual cost only increases from there the older you are.[15]
- Limited options — LTCI may be expensive for consumers, but it can also be expensive for companies that offer it. With fewer companies willing to take on that expense, the market narrows, meaning opportunities to price shop for policies with different options or custom benefits are limited.
- If you know you need it, you might not be able to get it — Insurance companies offering LTCI are taking on a risk that you may need LTCI. That risk is the foundation of the product — you may or may not need it. If you know you will need it because you have a dementia diagnosis or another illness for which you will need long-term care, you will likely not qualify for LTCI coverage.
- Use it or lose it — If you have LTCI and are in the minority of Americans who die having never needed long-term care, all the money you paid into your LTCI policy is gone.
- Possibly fluctuating rates — Your premium rate is not locked in on LTCI. Companies maintain the ability to raise or lower your premium amounts. This means some seniors face an ultimatum: Keep funding a policy at what might be a less affordable rate *or* lose coverage and let go of all the money they have paid so far.

---

[15] American Association for Long-Term Care Insurance. 2023. "Long-Term Care Insurance Facts – Data – Statistics – 2023 Reports" https://www.aaltci.org/long-term-care-insurance/learning-center/ltcfacts-2023.php

After that, you might be thinking, "How can people possibly be interested in LTCI?" But let me repeat myself — it's anticipated that as many as 70 percent of Americans will need long-term care. And although only one in ten Americans aged fifty-five-plus has purchased LTCI, keep in mind the high cost of nursing home care. Can you afford $7,000 a month to put into nursing home care and still have enough left over to help protect your legacy? This is a very real concern, considering one set of statistics reported a two-in-three chance that a senior citizen will become physically or cognitively impaired in their lifetime.[16] So, not to sound like a broken record, but it is vitally important to have a plan in place to deal with longevity and long-term care, especially if you intend to leave a financial legacy.

A few relevant statistics to keep in mind:
- The longer you live, the more health care you will likely need to pay for.
- The average cost of a private nursing home room in the United States between 2022 and 2023 was $9,034 a month.[17] But keep in mind, that is just the nursing home — it doesn't include other medical costs, let alone pleasantries like entertainment or hobby spending.
- As referenced earlier, Fidelity calculated in a 2022 study that a healthy couple retiring at age sixty-five could expect to pay around $315,000 over the course of retirement to cover health and medical expenses.

I know. "Whoa, there, Brad, I was hoping to have a realistic idea of health costs, not be driven over by a cement mixer!"

---

[16] payingforseniorcare.com. 2022. "Long-Term Senior Care Statistics" https://www.payingforseniorcare.com/statistics
[17] Chacour Koop. aPlaceforMom.com. September 15, 2023. "Average Cost of Long-Term Care: A State-by-State Guide to Senior Care in the U.S." https://www.aplaceformom.com/senior-living-data/articles/average-cost-long-term-care

The good news is, while we don't know these exact costs in advance, we know there *will* be costs. And you won't have to pay your total Medicare lifetime premiums in one day as a lump sum. Now that you have a good idea of health care costs in retirement, you can *plan* for them! That's the real point here: Planning in advance can keep you from feeling nickel-and-dimed to your wits' end. Instead, having a sizeable portion of your assets earmarked for health care can allow you the freedom to choose health care networks, coverage options, and long-term care possibilities that you like.

Product Riders

LTCI and self-funding are not the only ways to plan for the expenses of longevity. Some companies are getting creative with their products, particularly insurance companies. One way they are retooling to meet people's needs is through optional product riders on annuities and life insurance. Elsewhere in this book, I talk about annuity basics, but here's a brief overview: Annuities are insurance contracts. You pay the insurance company a premium — either as a lump sum or as a series of payments over a set amount of time — in exchange for guaranteed income payments.

One of the advantages of an annuity is it has access to riders, which allow you to tweak your contract for a fee — usually about 1 percent of the contract value annually. One annuity rider some companies offer is a long-term care rider. If you have an annuity with a long-term care rider and are not in need of long-term care, your contract behaves as any annuity contract would — nothing changes. In general, if you reach a point when you can't perform multiple functions of daily life on your own, you notify the insurance company, and if you meet the long-term care rider requirements, a representative will turn on those provisions of your contract to help you pay for your long-term care needs.

Like LTCI, different companies and products offer different options. Some annuity long-term care riders offer coverage of two years in a nursing home situation. Others cap expenses at two times the original annuity's value. It greatly depends. Some people prefer this option because there isn't a "use-it-or-lose-it" piece; if you die without ever having needed long-term care, you still will have had the income benefit from the base contract.

Still, as with any annuities or insurance contracts, there are the usual restrictions and limitations. Withdrawing money from the contract will affect future income payments, early distributions can result in a penalty, income taxes may apply, and, because the insurance company's solvency is what guarantees your payments, it's important to do your research about the insurance company you are considering purchasing a contract from.

Understandably, a discussion on long-term care is bound to feel at least a little tedious. Yet, this is an important piece of planning for income in retirement, particularly if you want to leave a legacy.

Spousal Planning

Here's one thing to keep in mind no matter how you plan to save: Many of us will be planning for more than ourselves. Look back at all the stats on health events and the likelihood of long life and long-term care. If they hold true for a single individual, then the likelihood of having a costly health or long-term care event is even higher for a married couple. You'll be planning for not just one life, but two. So, when it comes to long-term care insurance, annuities, self-funding, or whatever strategy you are looking at using, be sure you are funding longevity for the both of you.

Let's look at the example of Michael and Jessica. Both spouses retire around the same time, and they've done well saving for their known retirement expenses. Unfortunately, they don't plan for any of the "what ifs" that life throws at us. Early into their retirement, Michael passes away; now Jessica is down to one income. She does get to keep the higher of the two Social Security benefits, and Michael did have a pension, but the pension gets divided in half after his death. Jessica goes from being a married-filing-jointly tax return to a single tax return, which means her tax bill will increase even though her income has decreased drastically. Her monthly bills don't change much because she's still paying utilities and a mortgage for the same house. Instead of enjoying the comfortable retirement she and Michael planned, Jessica is now struggling.

It doesn't end there, however. Jessica is perfectly healthy right now, but if she suffers from an expensive illness or needs long-term care later in retirement, she may not have the resources to get the care she needs.

There were several things that Michael and Jessica could have done differently to help preserve assets in the event of the premature death of either spouse, including using resources such as long-term care or life insurance. A good planner can help you explore different options and scenarios to determine what is ideal for your situation.*

---

* This is a hypothetical example provided for illustrative purposes only; it does not represent a real life scenario, and should not be construed as advice designed to meet the particular needs of an individual's situation.

CHAPTER 2

Taxes

Where to begin with taxes? Perhaps by acknowledging we all bear responsibility for the resources we share such as. roads, bridges, and schools. Every American's patriotic duty is to pay their fair share of taxes. Many would agree with me. However, while they don't mind paying their fair share, they're not interested in paying one cent more than that!

Now, just talking about taxes probably takes your mind to April — tax season. You are probably thinking about all the forms you collect and how you file. Perhaps you are thinking about your certified public accountant or another qualified tax professional and saying to yourself, "I've already got taxes taken care of, thanks!"

However, what I see when people come into my office is that their relationship with their tax professional is purely a January through April relationship. That means they may have a tax *professional,* but not a tax *planner.*

What I mean is tax planning extends beyond filing taxes. In April, we are required to settle our accounts with the IRS to make sure we have paid up on our bill or even the score if we have overpaid. But real tax planning is about making each financial move in a way that allows you to keep the most money in your pocket and out of Uncle Sam's.

Now, as a caveat, I want to emphasize I am neither a CPA nor a tax planner, but I see the way taxes affect my clients, and I have plenty of experience helping clients implement tax-efficient strategies in their retirement plans in conjunction with their tax professionals.

It is especially important to me to help my clients develop tax-efficient strategies in their retirement plans because each dollar they can keep in their pockets is a dollar we can put to work.

Throughout our working years, we're encouraged to save, save, save into our 401(k). While there's nothing wrong with this (you should be saving!), most people don't realize that they're delaying the inevitable—paying taxes on those savings.

Most people agree that taxes will likely go up in the future, which means you're growing an asset that Uncle Sam will eventually start taking a bigger and bigger piece of once you begin taking distributions. What if you're married and your spouse passes away? Uncle Sam will take an even bigger cut because you've become a single filer instead of married-filing-jointly (Remember our couple, Michael and Jessica, from earlier?). And what if your children or grandchildren inherit your IRA or 401(k)? They'll have to pay taxes at their tax rate.

For most of us, a significant portion of our money for retirement ends up being our 401(k) or traditional IRAs, which are just waiting to be taxed. We call it the tax "time bomb" because we're just waiting for it to explode—and eventually, it will. This is why planning for taxes now is essential, especially while they are still on the lower side.

Think of it like this: When your favorite soda is on sale, you buy several at a time to get the best deal, right? You probably won't buy as much when it's not on sale. We should look at taxes the same way. When you can find a "sale" on taxes, you should consider taking advantage of it. For example, taxes are relatively low right now, making it a good time to contribute to an after-tax account such as a Roth IRA. Unlike a traditional IRA, which is tax-deferred, the money you contribute to a Roth is initially taxed at today's lower rate. So, when you begin taking qualified distributions (presumably when taxes are higher), none of that income will be taxed because you've *already paid* taxes on it previously. When taxes aren't advantageous, we want to use other accounts. This is where proper planning really comes into play.

The Fed

Now, in the United States, taxes can be a rather uncertain proposition. Depending on who is in the White House and which party controls Congress, we might be tempted to assume tax rates could either decline or increase in the next four to eight years accordingly. However, there is one (large!) factor we, as a nation, must confront: the national debt.

Currently, according to USDebtClock.org, we are over $34,000,000,000,000 in debt and climbing. That's $34 *trillion* with a "T." With just $1 trillion, you could park it in the bank at a zero percent interest rate and spend more than $54 million every day for fifty years without hitting a zero balance.

Even if Congress got a handle and stopped that debt from its daily compound, divided by each taxpayer, we each would owe about $264,000. So, will that be check, cash, or Venmo?[18]

My point here isn't to give you anxiety. I'm just cautioning you that even with the rosiest of outlooks on our personal income tax rates, none of us should count on low tax rates for the long term. Instead, you and your network of professionals (tax, legal, and financial) should constantly be looking for ways to take advantage of tax-saving opportunities as they come. After all, the most ideal "luck" is when proper planning meets opportunity.

So, how can we get started?

Know Your Limits

One of the foundational pieces of tax planning is knowing and understanding your marginal tax rate. Marginal tax rate is the

---

[18] usdebtclock.org. Accessed January 23, 2024.

tax rate you pay on your highest dollar of income. In the United States, we use a progressive tax system, meaning your marginal tax rate increases as your taxable income increases. However, to be clear, not all of your income is taxed at that highest rate — only the upper portion.

A taxpayer's income is divided into tax brackets, and the brackets determine the rate applied to increments of the filer's taxable income.

For example, if your single friend tells you she is in the 22 percent tax bracket, that means her highest amount of income is taxed at 22 percent, but chunks of her income are taxed at lower rates. Using the 2024 tax bracket below, her first $11,600 of income will be taxed at 10 percent, but her next chunk of income ($11,601 to $47,150) will be taxed at 12 percent. Finally, her income, beginning at $47,151, will be taxed at 22 percent. Her tax owed for the year — before any additional taxes or credits — is the accumulation of those three amounts.

\multicolumn{3}{c}{**2024 Tax Brackets: Single Filers**}
Tax Rate	**Taxable Income Bracket**	**Tax Owed**
10%	$0 to $11,600	10% of taxable income.
12%	$11,601 to $47,150	$1,160 plus 12% of the amount over $11,600
22%	$47,151 to $100,525	$5,426 plus 22% of the amount over $47,150
24%	$100,526 to $191,950	$17,168.50 plus 24% of the amount over $100,525
32%	$191,951 to $243,725	$39,110.50 plus 32% of the amount over $191,950
35%	$243,726 to $609,350	$55,678.50 plus 35% of the amount over $243,725
37%	$609,351 or more	$183,647.25 plus 37% of the amount over $609,350

[19]

It's important to note the difference between marginal and effective tax rates. The effective tax rate represents the percentage of taxable income an individual pays in taxes. To calculate the effective rate, take the total dollar amount you pay in income tax and divide it by your total income. Thus, it is the average rate and is almost always a lower percentage than a marginal rate.

Why are marginal and effective rates important in retirement planning? Federal income tax is one of the biggest

---

[19] Sabrina Parys and Tina Orem. Nerdwallet. November 14, 2023. "2023-2024 Tax Brackets and Federal Income Tax Rates" https://www.nerdwallet.com/article/taxes/federal-income-tax-brackets

expenses individuals pay in their lives. In some cases, the lifetime amount can exceed lifetime mortgage payments. Although there are federal tax breaks for Americans over the age of sixty-five, many former high-income earners continue to pay income taxes. Estimating your marginal tax rate is one of the components in determining when to begin Social Security and a crucial factor regarding Roth IRA conversions. Also, a thorough analysis of current and future marginal tax rates is important in the strategic planning for required minimum distributions (RMDs) on tax-deferred retirement accounts.

Assuming a Lower Tax Rate

Retirement has always been imagined as a time when you stop working and no longer earn wages or self-employment income. In the past, Social Security benefits were not subject to taxation. Even though pensions were usually taxable, their income stream didn't fully replace a recipient's previous salary. If you needed to pull from your investment funds during retirement, keep in mind that the principal had already been taxed. In general, prior to the 1970s, your income during retirement — your cash inflow — was usually taxed at a lower rate than when you were working because you had less income and certain portions of it were not taxable.

In 1978, lawmakers created Section 401 of the Internal Revenue Code to prevent companies from using tax-advantaged profit-sharing plans to primarily benefit executives. However, businessman Ted Benna reimagined this code as the foundation of the modern 401(k). This innovation ultimately led to the decline of traditional company pension plans, while shifting both control and risk to employees. The most significant change was the shift of taxation from when employees were paid and when investment income was earned to the time of withdrawal. This tax advantage encouraged individuals to save more money in tax-deferred plans than they would have in regular savings accounts, up to the allowed limits.

In addition, in 1983, Social Security introduced new tax brackets to address the problem of decreasing reserves. This resulted in both the potential for Social Security to become taxable and a significant shift in retirement planning strategy. Within a five-year period, the retirement planning landscape changed for decades going forward, possibly forever.

A big selling point for qualified retirement accounts (401(k)s, 403(b)s, IRAs, etc.) is the theory that people will pay less in tax during their retirement years than during their working years when they're putting that money away. The idea is that you're allowed to "defer" paying the tax on that income until your marginal tax rate drops in retirement. Hence, you pay less in tax on that income.

But what if it doesn't pan out that way? For some retirees, their marginal tax rate will stay the same in retirement or even increase. If you have a healthy balance in your qualified retirement account, combining its RMDs or even a Roth conversion with Social Security can result in what is called the "tax torpedo." This tax increase occurs when a larger percent of your Social Security becomes taxable, and that same income increase consequently bumps a taxpayer up to a higher marginal rate.

401(k)/IRA/Roth IRA

One sometimes-unexpected piece of tax planning in retirement concerns the 401(k) or IRA. Most of us have one of these accounts or an equivalent. We pay in throughout our working lives, dutifully socking away a portion of our earnings in these tax-deferred accounts. There's the rub: tax-*deferred*, not tax-*free*. Very rarely is anything free of taxation when you get down to it. Using 401(k)s and IRAs in retirement is no different. The taxes the government deferred when you were in your working years are now coming due, and you will pay taxes on that income at whatever your current tax rate is.

Just to ensure Uncle Sam gets his due, the government also has an RMD rule. Beginning at age seventy-three (or seventy-five if you were born in 1960 or after), you are required to withdraw a certain minimum amount every year from your 401(k) or IRA, or else you will face a tax penalty on any RMD monies you should have withdrawn but didn't — and that's on top of income tax. The SECURE Act 2.0 reduced the penalty to 25 percent (from 50 percent). Timely corrections also can further reduce the penalty to 10 percent.[20]

Of course, there is also the Roth account. You can think of the difference between a Roth and a traditional retirement account as the difference between taxing the seed and taxing the harvest. Because Roths get funded with post-tax dollars, there aren't tax penalties for early withdrawals of the principal, nor are there taxes on the growth after you reach age fifty-nine-and-one-half. Perhaps best of all, there are no RMDs. Of course, you must own a Roth account for a minimum of five years before you are able to take advantage of all its features.

This is one more area where it pays to be aware of your marginal tax rate. Some people may opt to put any excess RMDs from their traditional retirement accounts into stocks or insurance. Others may find it advantageous to "convert" their traditional retirement account funds to Roth account funds in a year during which they are in a lower tax bracket.

Roth IRA Conversions

A Roth conversion simply means converting (or withdrawing) monies from your traditional, tax-deferred retirement accounts and moving them to a Roth account. Once inside the Roth, any growth on these funds will accumulate completely tax-free, and tax will not be owed when the Roth funds are withdrawn assuming the conditions noted above. This is an exciting opportunity for accumulation! However, a thoughtful strategy

---

[20] Jim Probasco. Investopedia.com. January 6, 2023. "SECURE 2.0 Act of 2022." https://www.investopedia.com/secure-2-0-definition-5225115

is beneficial in the conversion process. Since dollars were placed into the traditional account pre-tax and the growth is taxable in these accounts, tax is owed on *all* the money converted to the Roth. Converting an employer plan account to a Roth IRA is a taxable event. Increased taxable income from the Roth IRA conversion may have several consequences, including (but not limited to) a need for additional tax withholding or estimated tax payments, the loss of certain tax deductions and credits, higher taxes on Social Security benefits, and higher Medicare premiums.

Points to consider regarding a conversion:

How are you going to pay the tax? Again, any time you withdraw funds from a 401(k) or traditional IRA, tax is owed on 100 percent of that money, whether the distribution was a basic withdrawal, an RMD, or a Roth conversion. In addition to the income tax, if the account owner is younger than fifty-nine-and-one-half, it is most likely a 10 percent tax penalty will be accessed. So, if you're under fifty-nine-and-one-half and have a year when your income is lower – reducing your marginal tax rate – you need to weigh the amount of the tax penalty against the decrease in ordinary income tax.

As a tricky sidenote, if you are under fifty-nine-and-one-half and you have tax withheld from your conversion and sent directly to the government, you will not escape the 10 percent penalty.

Did you compare your current tax rate to your estimated future rate? As mentioned above, a good time to consider a Roth is in a year when your taxable income — and thus your marginal tax rate — is lower than normal or lower than expected in the future. A popular conversion strategy is to transfer funds during a period referred to as "the trough years." That is the period after you've retired but before you begin receiving Social Security or are required to begin RMDs. It is easier to manage the tax on the conversion during these years as you have more control over the sources and the amounts of your income.

What is your Roth withdrawal strategy? There are four considerations here.

- Can you leave converted money in the Roth for at least five years? You must leave your converted money in the Roth for at least five years for the withdrawals to be tax-free. That five-year countdown begins on January 1 of the year you made the conversion, even if your conversion date was December 31. This five-year countdown applies in each year you make a conversion.
- Even if you hold the Roth funds for five years, you will still face penalties for withdrawals if you're under fifty-nine-and-one-half.[21]
- The longer you leave funds inside the Roth after the conversion, the more time it can grow and potentially recoup the tax levied on your traditional account's withdrawals. Remember, this money is now growing tax-free. A long growth period may be able to outweigh a loss in your balance due to income tax withholdings at conversion time. Also, an error in estimates of future tax rate margins (i.e., your future rates turned out to be less than the conversion year) can be made up by holding funds in your Roth for many years.[22]
- Planning to use your Roth as a legacy planning tool? There are various rules and options depending on the type of heir, but in most cases the Roth is given additional time to grow tax-free.

---

[21] Kailey Hagen. The Motley Fool. November 16, 2022. "4 Things to Know If You're Considering a Roth IRA Conversion This Year" https://www.fool.com/retirement/2022/11/16/4-things-to-know-if-youre-considering-a-roth-ira-c/

[22] Tim Steffen. Baird Wealth. October 16, 2023. "The Three Tests Before a Roth Conversion" https://www.bairdwealth.com/insights/wealth-management-perspectives/2023/09/the-three-tests-before-a-roth-conversion/

Does that make your head spin? Understandable. That's why it's so important to work with a financial professional and tax planner who can help you execute these sorts of tax-efficient strategies and help you understand what you are doing and why.

CHAPTER 3

Market Volatility

Up and down. Roller coaster. Merry-go-round. Bulls and bears. Peak-to-trough.
Sound familiar? This is the language we use to talk about the stock market. With volatility and spikes, even our language is jarring, bracing, and vivid.

Still, financial strategies tend to revolve around market-based products, and for good reasons. For one thing, there is no other financial class that packs the same potential for growth, pound for pound, as stock-based products. Because of growth potential, inflation challenges, and new opportunities, it may be unwise to avoid the market entirely.

However, along with the potential for growth is the potential for loss. At the time this book was written, many of the people I've seen in my office came in feeling uneasy because of the economic fallout of the COVID-19 outbreak of 2020, followed by the economic downturn and the inflation spike that happened in 2022.

So, how do we balance these factors? How do we try to satisfy both the need for protection and the need for growth?

For one thing, it is important to recognize the value of diversity. Now, I'm not just talking about the diversity of assets among different kinds of stocks, or even different kinds of stocks and bonds. That's only one kind of diversity. Stocks and bonds, though different, are both still important market-based products. Even within a diverse portfolio, most market-based products tend to rise or fall as a whole, just like an incoming tide. Therefore, a portfolio diverse in only market-sourced products won't automatically preserve your assets during times when the market declines.

In addition to the sort of "horizontal diversity" you have by purchasing a variety of stocks and bonds from different companies, I also suggest you think about "vertical diversity," or diversity among asset classes. This means having different product types, including securities products, bank products, and insurance products — with varying levels of growth potential, liquidity, and protection — all in accordance with your unique situation, goals, and needs.

However, it is crucial to determine your risk tolerance before deciding what products are ideal for you. Often, when clients first come to see me, I find their stated risk tolerance is completely at odds with how their portfolio is structured. Sometimes, they're not taking on enough risk. More often, they're taking on way too much. How do we fix this? We start by getting down to the nitty-gritty and determining at what point they are not willing to lose any more money. Remember, while there is always a risk of loss associated with the stock market, I believe it's still better to invest some money than to not invest at all—as long as you're comfortable with the amount you invest.

When investing, it really comes down to the math. Let's say you have $1 million saved for retirement. Are you comfortable potentially losing $100,000, $200,000, or $250,000? How would that potential loss impact your lifestyle? For some, it might mean slightly tightening the purse strings for a little while. For others, it might mean a significant change in their lifestyle. It varies from person to person. As I like to say, at what point are you killing your husband for allowing you to be in the stock market?

As a financial advisor, my job is to help you not panic and understand that even in times of volatility, there's still potential value in being in the market. We love to have assets that we want to grow in the market, but we know that risk is real. So, we try to determine a dollar amount you're comfortable putting at risk and hold you to that number. We keep note of this amount in your file, and when the market fluctuates, we can refer to the plan we made for this very situation. When we give you recommendations based on these plans, you are, in essence, taking your own advice.

The Color of Money

When you're looking at the overall diversity of your portfolio, part of the equation is knowing which products fit in what category: what has liquidity, what has asset preservation, and what has growth potential.

Before we dive in, keep in mind these aren't absolutes. You might think of liquidity, growth, and asset preservation as primary colors. While some products will look pretty much yellow, red, or blue, others will have a mix of characteristics, making them more green, orange, or purple.

Growth

I like to think of the growth category as red. It's powerful, it's somewhat volatile, and it's also the category where we have the greatest opportunities for growth and loss. Often, products in the growth category will have a good deal of liquidity but very little protection. These are our market-based products and strategies, and we think of them mostly in shades of red and orange to designate their growth and liquidity. This is usually a good place to be when you're young — think fast cars and flashy leather jackets — but its allure often wanes as you move closer to retirement. Examples of "red" products include:

- Stocks
- Equities
- Exchange-traded funds
- Mutual funds
- Corporate bonds
- Real estate investment trusts

- Speculations
- Alternative investments

Liquidity

Yellow is my liquid category color. I typically recommend having at least enough yellow money to cover six months' to a year's worth of expenses in case of emergency. Yellow assets don't need a lot of growth potential; they just need to be readily available when we need them. The "yellow" category includes assets like:

- Cash
- Money market accounts

Asset Preservation

The color of asset preservation, to me, is blue, which can incorporate products such as annuities. Tranquil, sure — even if it lacks a certain amount of flash. This is the direction I like to see people generally move toward as they're nearing retirement. The red, flashy look of stock market returns and the risk of possible overnight losses are less attractive as we near retirement and look for more consistency and reliability. While this category doesn't come with a lot of liquidity, the products here are backed by an insurance company, a bank, or a government entity. "Blue" products include things such as:

- Certificates of deposit (backed by banks)
- Government-based bonds (backed by the U.S. government)
- Life insurance (backed by insurance companies)
- Annuities (backed by insurance companies)

It is important to remember that the stock market is what it is. It goes up and down. So, assets that we're comfortable going backward on (losing money) are the same assets that we hope will go up in the long run. We just have to be willing and able to ride out the storm.

My philosophy is, if you can afford to risk some money and are comfortable with risk, don't automatically jump off the ship when it rocks and goes backward because we know that *will* happen. We want to consider if it makes sense to keep those assets in the market because we think that's the most efficient place for your money to be. If you have $1 million, the market goes down, you lose $100,000, and then you call me to say you want out of the market—that tells me you shouldn't have more than $150,000 to $200,000 in the market. The rest should be in less volatile products.

Of course, there are times we have to look at your portfolio and say, "You can't afford to only make 3 or 4 percent on your investments. If you do, you're going to run out of money." So, there are times when we might have to encourage people to take on a bit more risk than they're mentally comfortable with; we just have to plan for it.

Think of it like a casino. The house always wins, so we want to be the house. The key is the house is mathematical, not emotional. If you make decisions based on emotions, you're going to lose. My job is to help account for those emotions without letting them drive your decisions.

401(k)s

I want to take a second to specifically address a product many retirees will be using to build their retirement income: the 401(k) and other retirement accounts. Any of these retirement accounts (IRAs, 401(k)s, 403(b)s, etc.) are basically "tax wrappers." What do I mean by that? Well, depending on your plan provider, a 401(k) could include target-date funds, passively managed products, stocks, bonds, mutual funds, or even variable, fixed, and fixed index annuities, all collected in one place and governed by rules (a.k.a. the "tax wrapper"). These rules govern how much money you can put inside, what ways you can put it in, when you will pay taxes on it, and when you can take the money out. Inside the 401(k), each of the products inside the "tax wrapper" might have its own fees or commissions, in addition to the management fee you pay on the 401(k) itself.

Now, fees can be troublesome. You can't get something for nothing, and fees are how many financial companies and professionals make a living. Yet, it's important to recognize even a fee with a fraction of a percentage point is money out of your pocket — money that represents not just the one-time fee of today but also an opportunity cost. For example, consider how a $100,000 IRA that earns 6 percent over a twenty-five-year period without investment fees would earn $430,000. But if just a 0.5 percent fee was factored into that investment, the IRA would be worth $379,000 in twenty-five years — a $50,500 decrease. For someone close to retirement, how much do you think fees may have cost over their lifetime?

Even for those close to retirement, it's important to look at management fees and assess if you think you're getting what you pay for. Over the course of ten years, those costs can add up, and you may have decades ahead of you in which you will need to rely on your assets.

Dollar-Cost Averaging

With 401(k)s and other market-based retirement products, dollar-cost averaging is a concept that can work in your favor when you are investing for the long term. When the market is trending up, if you are consistently paying in money, month over month, great; your investments can grow, and you are adding to your assets. When the market takes a dip, no problem; your dollars buy more shares at a lower price. At some point, we hope the market will rebound, in which case your shares can grow and possibly be more valuable than they were before. This concept is what we call "dollar-cost averaging." While it can't ensure a profit or guarantee against losses, it's a time-tested strategy for investing in a volatile market.

However, when you are in retirement, this strategy may work against you. You may have heard of "reverse" dollar-cost averaging. Before, when the market lost ground, you were "bargain-shopping"; your dollars purchased more assets at a reduced price. When you are in retirement, you are no longer the purchaser; you are selling. So, in a down market, you have to sell more assets to make the same amount of money as what you made in a favorable market.

I've had lots of people step into my office to talk to me about this, emphasizing how their advisor says, "the market always bounces back, and I have to just hold on for the long term."

There's some basis for this thinking; thus far, the market has always rebounded to higher heights than before. But this is no guarantee, and the prospect of potentially higher returns in five years may not be very helpful in retirement if you are relying on the income from those returns to pay this month's electric bill, for example.

Is There a "Perfect" Product?

To bring us back around to the discussion of asset preservation, growth, and liquidity, the ideal product would be a "ten" in all three categories, right? Completely guaranteed, doubling in size every few years, and accessible whenever you want. Does such a product exist? Absolutely not.

Instead of running in circles looking for that perfect product, the silver bullet, the unicorn of financial strategies, it's more important to circle back to the concept of a balanced, asset-diverse portfolio.

This is why it could be prudent to work with a knowledgeable financial professional who knows what various financial products can do and ways to use them in your personal retirement strategy.*

---

* Investing involves risk, including the potential loss of principal. No investment strategy can guarantee a profit or protect against loss in periods of declining values. Any references to protection benefits or

guaranteed/lifetime income streams refer only to fixed insurance products, not securities or investment products. Insurance and annuity product guarantees are backed by the financial strength and claims-paying ability of the issuing insurance company.

CHAPTER 4

Retirement Income

Retirement. For many of us, it's what we've saved for and dreamed of, pinning our hopes to a magical someday. Is that someday full of traveling? Is it filled with grandkids? Gardening? Maybe your fondest dream is simply never having to work again, never having to clock in or be accountable to someone else.

Your ability to do these things all hinges on *income*. Without the money to support these dreams, even a basic level of work-free lifestyle is unsustainable. That's why planning for your income in retirement is so foundational. But where do we begin?

It's easy to feel overwhelmed by this question. Some may feel the urge to amass a large lump sum and then try to put it all in one product — insurance, investments, liquid assets — to provide all the growth, liquidity, and income they need. Instead, I think you need a more balanced approach. After all, retirement planning isn't magic. As I mention elsewhere, there is no single product that can be all things to all people (or even all things to one person). No approach works unilaterally for everyone. That's why it's important to talk to a financial professional who can help you lay down the basics and take you step-by-step through the process. Not only will you have the assurance you have addressed the areas you need to, but you will also have an ally who can help you break down the process and help keep you from feeling overwhelmed.

Sources of Income

Thinking of all the pieces of your retirement expenses might be intimidating. But, like cleaning out a junk drawer or revisiting that garage remodel, once you have laid everything out, you can begin to sort things into categories.

Once you have a good overall picture of where your expenses will lie, you can start stacking up the resources to cover them.

Social Security

Social Security is a guaranteed, inflation-adjusted federal insurance program that plays a significant part in most of our retirement plans. From delaying until you've reached full retirement age or beyond to examining spousal benefits, as I discuss elsewhere in this book, there is plenty you can do to try to make the most of this monthly benefit. As with all your retirement income sources, it's important to consider ways to make this resource stretch to provide the most bang and buck for your situation.

Pension

Another generally reliable source of retirement income for you might be a pension, if you are one of the lucky people who still has one.

If you don't have a pension, go ahead and skim on to the next section. If you do have a pension, keep on reading.

Because your pension can be such a central piece of your retirement income plan, you will want to put some thought into answering basic questions about it.

How well is your pension funded? Since the heyday of the pension plan, companies and governments have neglected to fund their pension obligations, causing a persistent problem with this otherwise reliable asset.

Consider the factors at play, though. Pensions had been underfunded and gained a boost from strong market performance, most recently in 2021.[23] What happens to the solvency of those pension funds if the market declines?

It can be worthwhile to keep tabs on your pension's health and know what your options are for withdrawing from it. Typically, you have one chance at electing the distribution option at your retirement with no recourse to change at a later date, so you will want to look at all options before making a final decision. If you have already retired and made those decisions, this may be a foregone conclusion. If not, it pays to know what you can expect and what decisions you can make, such as taking spousal options to cover your spouse if they outlive you.

Also, some companies are incentivizing lump-sum payouts of pensions to reduce the companies' payment liabilities. If that's the case with your employer, talk to your financial professional to see if it might be prudent to do something like that or if it might be better to stick with lifetime payments or other options.

Your 401(k) and IRA

One "modern way" to save for retirement is in a 401(k) or IRA (or their nonprofit or governmental equivalents). These tax-advantaged accounts are, in my opinion, a poor substitute for pensions, but one of the biggest disservices we do to ourselves is not taking full advantage of them in the first place. While the average 401(k) balance for Americans between the ages of forty and forty-nine is $105,500, the median account balance is

---

[23] pewtrusts.org. November 8, 2023. "Public Retirement Systems Need Sustainable Policies to Navigate Volatile Financial Markets" https://www.pewtrusts.org/en/research-and-analysis/issue-briefs/2023/11/public-retirement-systems-need-sustainable-policies-to-navigate-volatile-financial-markets

much lower. The median, which separates half of accounts with higher balances and half with lower balances, is just $34,100.[24]

Also, if you have changed jobs over the years, do the work of tracking down any benefits from your past employers. You might have an IRA here or a 401(k) there; keep track of those so you can pull them together and look at those assets when you're ready to look at establishing sources of retirement income.

Do You Have ...

- Life insurance?
- Annuities?
- Long-term care insurance?
- Any passive income sources?
- Stock and bond portfolios?
- Liquid assets? (What's in your bank account?)
- Alternative investments?
- Rental properties?

If you are going through the work of sitting with a financial professional, it's important to look at your full retirement income picture and pull together *all* your assets, no matter how big or small. From the free insurance policy offered at your bank to the sizable investment in your brother-in-law's modestly successful furniture store, you want to have a good idea of where your money is.

You might be thinking to yourself, "Brad, this is common sense. Of course, I know where all my money is."

And yet, it is not uncommon for people to over- or underestimate how much they have saved and how much it will take to live their desired lifestyle in retirement. For example, an older couple comes to see me, and they've managed to save a

---

[24] Cheyenne DeVon. cnbc.com. July 13, 2023. "Here's how much Americans in their 40s have in their 401(k)s" https://www.cnbc.com/2023/07/13/fidelity-how-much-americans-in-their-40s-have-in-their-401ks.html

considerable nest egg. They're hoping to retire within two years, and their goal is to have $2,000 a week for the rest of their lives. The husband is used to handling all the financials for the two of them and has done the math to determine what he thinks it will cost them to have that $2,000 a week, but he hasn't accounted for interest rates. At the time of writing this book, interest rates are considerably higher than they've been in the past, which is a good thing in this instance. It will actually take around $900,000 less than the couple thought for them to comfortably have that $2,000 a week. This example shows that people can often accomplish their goals with less than they think they need.

I also see the opposite happen, unfortunately. I've seen people with $500,000 who want to spend $50,000 a year out of it. Obviously, that's not sustainable, which is why it's so important to know where your money is so you know exactly how much you can (or can't) afford to spend in retirement.

Retirement Income Needs

How much income will you need in retirement? How do you determine that? A lot of people work toward a random number, thinking, "If I can just have a million dollars, I'll be comfortable in retirement!" Don't get me wrong; it is possible to save up a lot of money and then retire in the hopes you can keep your monthly expenses lower than some set estimation. But I think this carries a general risk of running out of money. Instead, I work with my clients to find out what their current and projected income needs are and then work from there to see how we might cover any gaps between what they have and what they want.

Goals and Dreams

I like to start with your pie in the sky. Do you find yourself planning for your vacations more thoroughly than you do your retirement? Maybe it's because planning a vacation is less stressful: Having a week at the beach go awry is, well, a walk on the beach compared to running out of money in retirement. Whatever the case, perhaps it would be better if you thought of your retirement as a vacation in and of itself — no clocking in, no boss, no overtime. If you felt unlimited by financial strain, what would you do?

Would an endless vacation for you mean Paris and Rome? Would it mean mentoring at children's clubs or serving at the local soup kitchen? Or maybe it would mean deepening your ties to those immediately around you — neighbors, friends, and family. Maybe it would mean more time to take part in the hobbies and activities you love. Have you been considering a second (or even third) act as a small-business owner, turning a hobby or passion into a revenue source?

This is your time to daydream and answer the question: If you could do anything, what would you do?

After that, it's a matter of putting a dollar amount on it. What are the costs of round-the-world travel? One couple I know said their highest priority in retirement was being able to take each of their grandchildren on a cross-country vacation every year. That's a pretty specific goal — one that is reasonably easy to nail down a budget for.

Another couple had a similar dream. They had four adult kids, and every year all five families would take a family vacation that Mom and Dad would pay for. Their vision was to somehow put their money to use even after they'd passed away so that all four children and their families could continue taking that vacation together every year. It's probably one of the most unique goals I've encountered. They ended up putting a trust in place that would specifically fund the family vacations even after Mom and Dad could no longer join in—they could still be with them in spirit.*

---

* This is a hypothetical example provided for illustrative purposes only; it does not represent a real life scenario, and should not be construed as advice designed to meet the particular needs of an individual's situation.

Current Budget

Compiling a current expense report is one of the trickiest pieces of retirement preparation. Many people assume the expenses of their lives in retirement will be lower. After all, there will be no drive to work, no need for a formal wardrobe, and — perhaps most impactful of all — no more saving for retirement!

Yet, we often underestimate our daily spending habits. That's why I typically ask my clients to bring in their bank statements for the past year — they are reflective of your *actual* spending, not just what you think you're spending.

Your expenses will tell us where to set your goal for retirement income. For instance, if I have $7,000 in monthly expenses, I'll need $7,000 in income. Knowing where your money is going will help us determine where it will come from. We'll also need to account for taxes, naturally, and the impact they will have to figure out exactly what is needed post-working years. It's a bit plug-and-play with the numbers to figure these calculations out, but at the end of the day, expenses drive income for everyone.

I can't count the number of times I have sat with a couple, asked them about their spending, and heard them throw out a number that seemed incredibly low. When I ask them where the number came from, they usually say they estimated based on their total bills. Yet, our spending is so much more than our mortgage, utilities, cable, phone, car, grocery, or credit card bills.

"What about clothes?" I ask, "Or dining out? What about gifts and coffees and last-minute birthday cards?" That's when the lights come on.

This is why I suggest collecting a year's worth of information. There is usually no such thing as a one-time purchase. Did you buy new furniture? Even if that is a rarity, do you think that will be the last time you *ever* buy furniture?

Another hefty expense is spending on the kids. Many of the couples I work with are quick to help their adult children, whether it's something like letting them live in the basement, paying for college, babysitting, paying an occasional bill, or contributing to a grandchild's college fund. Research concluded that 54 percent of those in the Gen Z and millennial age groups lean on parents for financial support. Among those, 23 percent are heavily supported by parents.[25]

My clients sometimes protest that what they do for their grown children can stop in retirement. They don't *need* to help. But I get it. Parents like to feel needed. And, while you never want to neglect saving for retirement in favor of taking on financial risks (like your child's student debt), the parents who help their adult children do so in part because it helps them feel fulfilled.

When it comes down to expenses, including (and especially) spending on your family, don't make your initial calculations based on what you *could* whittle your budget down to if you *had* to. Instead, start from where you are. Who wants to live off a bare-bones bank account in retirement?

Other Expenses

Once you have nailed down your current budget and your dreams or goals for retirement, there are a few other outstanding pieces to think about — some expenses many people don't take the time to consider before making and executing a plan. But I'm assuming you want to get it right, so let's take a look.

Housing

Do you know where you want to live in retirement? This makes up a substantial piece of your income puzzle — since the typical

---

[25] Experianpic.com. June 27, 2023. "Most Gen Zers and millennials still rely on parents for financial support and feel ashamed asking for help" https://www.experianplc.com/newsroom/press-releases/2023/most-gen-zers-and-millennials-still-rely-on-parents-for-financial-support-and-feel-ashamed-asking-for-help

American household owns a home, and it's generally their largest asset.

Some people prefer to live right where they are for as long as they can. Others have been waiting for retirement to pull the trigger on an ambitious move, like purchasing a new house, or even downsizing. Whatever your plans and whatever your reasons, there are quite a few things to consider.

Mortgage

Do you still have a mortgage? What may have been a nice tax boon in your working years could turn into a financial burden in your retirement. After all, when you are on a limited income, a mortgage is just one more bill sapping your financial strength. It is something to put some thought into, whether you plan to age in place or are considering moving to your dream home, buying a house out of state, or living in a retirement community.

Upkeep and Taxes

A house without a mortgage still requires annual taxes. While it's tempting to think of this as a once-a-year expense, when you have limited earning potential, your annual tax bill might be something into which you should put a little more forethought.

The costs of homeownership aren't just monetary. When you find yourself dealing with more house than you need, it can drain your time and energy. From keeping clutter at bay to keeping the lawn mower running, upkeep can be extensive and expensive. For some, that's a challenge they heartily accept and can comfortably take on. For others, the idea of yard work or cleaning an area larger than they need feels foolish.

For instance, Peggy discovered after her knee replacement that most of her house was inaccessible to her when she was laid up.

"It felt ridiculous to pay someone else to dust and vacuum a house I was only living in 40 percent of!"

Practicality and Adaptability

Erik and Marla are looking to retire within the next two decades. They just sold their old three-bedroom ranch-style house. Their twins are in high school, and the couple has wanted to "upgrade" for years. Now they live in a gorgeous 1940s three-story house with all the kitchen space they ever wanted, five sprawling bedrooms, and a library and media room for themselves and their children. Within months of moving in, the couple realized a house perfect for their active teens would no longer be perfect for them in five to fifteen years.

"We are paying the mortgage for this house, but we've started saving for the next one," said Marla, "because who wants to climb two flights of stairs to their bedroom when they're seventy-eight?"

Others I know have encountered a similar situation in their personal lives. After a health crisis, one couple found the luxurious tub for two they toiled to install had become a specter of a bad slip and a potential safety risk. It's important to think through what your physical reality could be. I always emphasize to my clients that they should plan for whatever their long-term future might hold, but it's amazing how many people don't give it much thought.

Contracts and Regulations

If you are looking into a cross-country move, be aware of new tax tables or local ordinances in the area where you are looking to move. After all, you don't want to experience sticker-shock when you are looking at downsizing or reducing your bills in retirement.

Along the same lines, if you are moving into a retirement community, be sure to look at the fine print. What happens if you must move into a different situation for long-term care? Will you be penalized? Will you be responsible for replacing your slot in the community? What are all the fees, and what do they cover?

Inflation

As I write this in 2024, America has experienced a wave of inflation following a lengthy period of low inflation. Inflation zoomed to 9.1 percent in June 2022, its highest mark since November 1981.[26] By the end of 2023, the inflation rate decreased to 3.1 percent.[27]

Core inflation is yet another measurement that excludes goods with prices that tend to be more volatile, such as food and energy costs. Core inflation for a twelve-month period ending in November 2023 was 4.0 percent. It so happened that energy prices decreased 5.4 percent over that timeframe.[28]

However, inflation isn't a one-time bump; it has a cumulative effect. Again, that can impact the price of groceries more than other goods. Even with relatively low inflation over the past few decades, for the purchasing power of $2 in 1997 equates to $3.82 today.[29] Want to go to a show? A $20 ticket in 1997 would cost $43.61 in 2023.[30]

What if we hit a stretch in retirement like the late seventies and early eighties, when annual inflation rates of 10 percent became the norm? It may be wise to consider some extra padding in your retirement income plan to account for any potential increase in inflation in the future.

---

[26] tradingeconomics.com. 2022 Data/2023 Forecast/1914-2021 Historical. "United States Inflation Rate" https://tradingeconomics.com/united-states/inflation-cpi

[27] statistica.com. December 13, 2023. "Monthly 12-month inflation rate in the United States from November 2020 to November 2023" https://www.statista.com/statistics/273418/unadjusted-monthly-inflation-rate-in-the-us

[28] U.S. Inflation Calculator. "United States Core Inflation Rates (1957-2022)" https://www.usinflationcalculator.com/inflation/united-states-core-inflation-rates/

[29] In2013dollars.com. "$2 in 1997 is worth $3.82 today" https://www.in2013dollars.com/us/inflation/1997?amount=2

[30] In2013dollars.com "Admission to movies, theaters, and concerts priced at $20 in 1997>$43.61 in 2023" https://www.in2013dollars.com/Admission-to-movies,-theaters,-and-concerts/price-inflation

Shrinkflation

Another important yet often overlooked factor to consider is called "shrinkflation." Essentially a form of hidden inflation, shrinkflation signifies a reduction in packaging while retaining a similar price as before.

For example, as you walk down a grocery store aisle, you spot your favorite pickles. The jar still costs the same — roughly $5 — and you add it to your cart. Then you get home, and the container seems different after digging out a few crispy dills. You examine the jar and discover it contains fewer ounces than previous jars you purchased. However, you paid roughly the same price for your pickles.

Now, move over to the aisle featuring salty snacks. You might notice a sale on a certain brand of chips, though you must buy three or four bags to receive a discount promoted by the store. You decide to purchase that many bags to capitalize on the lower price. When you get home, you notice the packaging is smaller than you anticipated. The deal you accepted may not have been as thrifty as you perceived.

Shrinkflation can be a way for companies to quietly boost, or retain, profit margins without having to change much else — essentially, they are simply charging the same price for less product. Companies do this because customers are more likely to spot price increases than size reductions. However, research has also shown that these shrinkflation tactics can backfire into negative consumer perceptions of their brands once they come to light. Who wants to pay the same for less, especially when they have already grown accustomed to getting more for their money's worth?[31]

---

[31] Daniel Liberto. Investopedia. November 16, 2023. "Shrinkflation: What It Is, Reasons for It, How to Spot It"
https://www.investopedia.com/terms/s/shrinkflation.asp

Aging

Also, in the expense category, think about longevity. We all hope to age gracefully. However, it's important to face the prospect of aging with a sense of realism.

For many families, the elephant in the room is long-term care. No one wants to admit they will likely need it, but estimates indicate almost 70 percent of us will.[32] Aging is a significant piece of retirement income planning because you'll want to figure out how to set aside money for your care, either at home or away from it. The more comfortable you get with discussing your wishes and plans with your loved ones, the easier planning for the financial side of it can be.

I denote health care and potential long-term care costs in more detail elsewhere in this book, but suffice it to say nursing home care tends to be very expensive and typically isn't something you get to choose when you will need.

It isn't just the costs of long-term care that pose a concern in living longer. It's also about covering the possible costs of everything else associated with living longer. For instance, if Henry retires from his job as a biochemical engineer at age sixty-five, perhaps he plans to have a very decent income for twenty years until he turns eighty-five. But what if he lives until he's ninety-five? That's a whole third — ten years — more of personal income he will need.

Putting It All Together

Whew! So, you have pulled together what you have, and you have a pretty good idea of where you want to be. Now, you and your financial professional can go about the work of arranging what assets you *have* to cover what you *need* — and how you might try to cover any gaps.

---

[32] Moll Law Group. 2022. "The Cost of Long-Term Care" https://www.molllawgroup.com/the-cost-of-long-term-care.html

Like the proverbial man in the Bible who built his house on a rock, I like to help my clients figure out ways to cover their day-to-day living expenses — their needs — with insurance and other guaranteed income sources like pensions and Social Security.

When helping clients determine if and when they can afford to retire, I follow what I call the C.L.I.M.B. Process. C.L.I.M.B. stands for Conserve and Grow Assets, Lifetime Income, Insure Your Health, Minimize Taxes, and Build a Legacy—all the major areas your retirement plan should address to help you reach the heights of financial independence.

Again, you should keep in mind there isn't one single financial vehicle, asset, or source to fill all your needs, and that's okay. One of the challenges of planning for your income in retirement concerns figuring out what products and strategies to use. You can release some of that stress when you accept the fact you will probably need a diverse portfolio — potentially with bonds, stocks, insurance, and other income sources — not just one massive money pile.

One way to help shore up your income gaps is by working with your financial professional and a qualified tax advisor to help mitigate your tax exposure. If you have a 401(k) or IRA, a tax advisor in your corner may be able to help you figure out how and when to take distributions from your account in a way that doesn't push you into a higher tax bracket. Or you might learn ways to use tax-advantaged bonds more effectively. Effective tax planning isn't necessarily about "adding" to your income. Especially regarding retirement, it's less about what you make than it is about what you keep. Paying a lower tax bill keeps more money in your pocket, which is where you want it when it comes to retirement income.

Now you can look at ways to cover your remaining retirement goals. Are there products like long-term care insurance specific to a certain kind of expense you anticipate? Is there a particular asset you want to use for your "play" money — money for trips and gifts for the grandkids? Is there any way you can portion off money for those charitable legacy plans?

Once you have analyzed your income wants, needs, and the assets necessary to realistically cover them, you may have a gap. The masterstroke of a competent financial professional will be to help you figure out how you will cover that gap. Will you need to cut out a round of golf a week? Maybe skip the new car? Or will you need to take more substantial action?

One way to cover an income gap is to consider working longer or even part-time before retirement and even after that magical calendar date. This may not be the best "plan" for you; disabilities, work demands, and physical or emotional limitations can hinder the best-laid plans to continue working. However, if it is physically possible for you, this is one considerable way to help your assets last for more than one reason.

In fact, 55 percent of the Americans responding to a survey report they plan to work part-time after retiring, while 15 percent expect compensation from work to be their primary source of retirement income.[33]

I work with a lot of clients who come in thinking they'll never be able to retire. Yet once we've gone through the C.L.I.M.B. Process and developed a financial plan that accounts for all the different areas they'll need to take into consideration, clients typically feel much better after seeing where they stand and knowing where to go from there.

When you're retired, you no longer have an employer paying you a steady check. It is up to you to make sure you have saved and planned for the income you need. A trusted financial advisor can help you do just that.

---

[33] Kerry Hannon. Yahoo!finance.com. July 15, 2023. "Future retirees plan to work longer, partly due to savings shortfalls" https://finance.yahoo.com/news/future-retirees-plan-to-work-longer-partly-due-to-savings-shortfalls-160038419.html

CHAPTER 5

Social Security

Social Security is often the foundation of retirement income. Backed by the strength of the U.S. Treasury, it provides perhaps the most dependable paycheck you will have in retirement.

From the time you collect your first paycheck from the job that made you a bona fide taxpayer, you are paying into the grand old Social Security system. What grew and developed out of the pressures of the Great Depression has become one of the most popular government programs in the country, and if you pay in for the equivalent of ten years or more, you, too, can benefit from the Social Security program.

Now, before we get into the nitty-gritty of Social Security, I'd like to address a current concern: Will Social Security still be there for you when you reach retirement age?

The Future of Social Security

This question is ever-present as headlines trumpet an underfunded Social Security program, alongside the sea of baby boomers retiring in droves and the comparatively smaller pool of younger people who are funding the system.

The Social Security Administration itself acknowledges this concern as each Social Security statement now contains a link to its website (ssa.gov) and a page entitled, "Will Social Security Be There For Me?"

Just a reminder, as if you needed one, that nothing in life is guaranteed. Additionally, depending on who you're listening to, Social Security funds may run low before 2034, thanks to the financial instability and government spending that accompanied the 2020 COVID-19 pandemic.

Before you get too discouraged, though, here are a few thoughts to keep you going:

- Even if the program is only paying 75-78 cents on the dollar for scheduled benefits, this is notably not zero.
- The Social Security Administration has made changes in the distant and near past to help protect the fund's solvency, including increasing retirement ages and striking certain filing strategies.
- There are many changes Congress could make, and lawmakers routinely discuss ways to fix the system, such as further increasing full retirement age and eligibility.
- One thing no one is seriously discussing? Reneging on current obligations to retirees or the soon-to-retire.

Take heart. The real answer to the question, "Will Social Security be there for me?" is still yes.

This question is important to consider when you look at how much we, as a nation, rely on this program. Did you know Social Security benefits replace about 40 percent of a person's original income when they retire?[34]

If you ask me, that's a pretty significant piece of your retirement income puzzle.

Another caveat? You may not realize this, but no one can legally "advise" you about your Social Security benefits.

"But, Brad," you may be thinking, "isn't that part of what you do? And what about that nice gentleman at the Social Security Administration office I spoke with on the phone?"

---

[34] ssa.gov. "Alternate Measure of Replacement Rates for Social Security Benefits and Retirement Income"
https://www.ssa.gov/policy/docs/ssb/v68n2/v68n2p1.html.

Don't get me wrong. Social Security Administration employees know their stuff. They are trained to understand policies and programs, and they are usually pretty quick to tell you what you can and cannot do. But the government specifically stipulates that because Social Security is a benefit you alone have paid into and earned. Your Social Security decisions are *also* yours alone.

When it comes to financial professionals, we can't push you in any direction, but — there's a big but here — working with a well-informed financial professional is still incredibly handy for your Social Security decisions. Why? Because someone who's worth their salt will know what withdrawal strategies might pertain to your specific situation and will ask questions that can help you determine what you are looking for when it comes to your Social Security.

For instance, some people want the highest possible monthly benefit. Others want to start their benefits early, and not always because of financial need. I heard about one man who called in to start his Social Security payments the day he qualified just because he liked to think of it as the government paying back a debt it owed him, and he enjoyed the feeling of receiving a check from Uncle Sam.

Whatever your reasons, questions, or feelings regarding Social Security, the decision is yours alone, but working with a financial professional can help you put your options in perspective by showing you — both with industry knowledge and with proprietary software or planning processes — where your benefits fit into your overall strategy for retirement income.

One reason the federal government doesn't allow for "advice" related to Social Security, I suspect, is so no one can profit from giving you advice related to your Social Security benefit — or from providing any clarifications. Again, this is a sign of an experienced financial professional. Those who are passionate about their work will be knowledgeable about what benefit strategies might be to your advantage and will happily share those possible options with you.

Full Retirement Age

When it comes to Social Security, it seems like many people only think so far as "yes." They don't take the time to understand the various options available. Instead, because it is common knowledge you can begin your benefits at age sixty-two, that's what many of us do. While more people are opting to delay taking benefits, age sixty-two is still a popular age to start.[35]

Some people fail to understand that starting benefits early may leave significant money on the table. You see, the Social Security Administration bases your monthly benefit on two factors: your earnings history and your full retirement age (FRA).

From your earnings history, the SSA pulls the thirty-five years you made the most money and uses a mathematical indexing formula to figure out a monthly average from those years. If you paid into the system for less than thirty-five years, then every year you didn't pay in will be counted as a zero.

Once they have calculated what your monthly earnings would be at FRA, the government then calculates what to put on your check based on how close you are to FRA. FRA was originally set at sixty-five, but as the population aged and lifespans lengthened, the government shifted FRA later and later, based on an individual's year of birth. Check out the following chart to see when you will reach FRA.[36]

---

[35] Emily Brandon, Erica Sandberg. U.S. News & World Report. August 14, 2023. "The Most Popular Ages to Collect Social Security" https://money.usnews.com/money/retirement/social-security/articles/the-most-popular-ages-to-collect-social-security

[36] Social Security Administration. "Full Retirement Age" https://www.ssa.gov/planners/retire/retirechart.html

Age to Receive Full Social Security Benefits*

(Called "full retirement age" [FRA] or "normal retirement age.")

Year of Birth*	FRA
1937 or earlier	65
1938	65 and 2 months
1939	65 and 4 months
1940	65 and 6 months
1941	65 and 8 months
1942	65 and 10 months
1943-1954	66
1955	66 and 2 months
1956	66 and 4 months
1957	66 and 6 months
1958	66 and 8 months
1959	66 and 10 months
1960 and later	67

*If you were born on January 1 of any year, you should refer to the previous year. (If you were born on the 1st of the month, we figure your benefit [and your full retirement age] as if your birthday was in the previous month.)[37]

When you reach FRA, you are eligible to receive 100 percent of whatever the Social Security Administration calculates as your full monthly benefit.

Starting at age sixty-two, for every year before FRA you claim benefits, your monthly check is reduced by 5 percent or more. Conversely, for every year you delay taking benefits past FRA, your monthly benefit increases by 8 percent (until age seventy — after that, there is no monetary advantage to delaying Social Security benefits). While your circumstances and needs may vary, a lot of financial professionals still urge people to at least consider delaying until they reach age seventy.

Why wait?[38]

Taking benefits early could affect your monthly check by _____.								
62	63	64	65	66	FRA 67	68	69	70
-30%	-25%	-20%	-13.3%	-6.7%	0	+8%	+16%	+24%

[39]

My Social Security

If you are over thirty, you have probably received a notice from the Social Security Administration telling you to activate something called "My Social Security." This is a handy way to learn more about your particular benefit options, keep track of your earnings record, and calculate the benefits you have accrued over the years.

Essentially, My Social Security is an online account you can activate to see your personal Social Security picture. You can

---

[37] Social Security Administration. 2023. "Normal Retirement Age" https://www.ssa.gov/oact/progdata/nra.html
[38] Social Security Administration. 2024. "Retirement Benefits" https://www.ssa.gov/pubs/EN-05-10035.pdf
[39] Social Security Administration. 2023. "Effect of Early or Delayed Retirement on Retirement Benefits" https://www.ssa.gov/oact/ProgData/ar_drc.html

access this information at www.ssa.gov/myaccount. This can be extremely helpful when it comes to planning for income in retirement and figuring out the difference between your anticipated income versus anticipated expenses.

COLA

Social Security is a largely guaranteed piece of the retirement puzzle: If you get a statement that reads you should expect $1,000 a month, you can be sure you will receive $1,000 a month. But there is one variable detail, and that is something called the cost-of-living adjustment (COLA).

The COLA is an increase in your monthly check meant to address inflation in everyday life. After all, your expenses will likely continue to experience inflation in retirement, but you will no longer have the opportunity for raises, bonuses, or promotions you had when you were working. Instead, Social Security receives an annual cost-of-living increase tied to the Department of Labor's Consumer Price Index for Urban Wage Earners and Clerical Workers (CPI-W). If the CPI-W measurement shows inflation rose a certain amount for regular goods and services, then Social Security recipients will see that reflected in their COLA.

COLA adjustments have climbed as high as 14.3 percent (1980), and in 2023, they reached 8.7 percent — the largest increase in more than forty years. In a no- or low-inflation environment (such as in 2010, 2011, and 2016), Social Security recipients will not receive an adjustment.[40] The 2024 adjustment decreased to 3.2 percent.[41] Some view the COLA as a perk, bump, or bonus, but in reality, it works more like this: Your mom sends you to the store with $2.50 for a gallon of milk. Milk costs exactly $2.50. The next week, you go back with that same amount, but it is now $2.52 for a gallon, so you go back to

---

[40] ssa.gov. "Cost-Of-Living Adjustments" ssa.gov/oact/cola/colaseries.html
[41] ssa.gov. "Cost-of-Living Adjustment (COLA) Information for 2024" https://www.ssa.gov/cola/

Mom, and she gives you 2 cents. You aren't bringing home more milk — it just costs more money.

The COLA is less about "making more money" and more about keeping seniors' purchasing power from eroding when inflation is a big factor. Still, don't let that detract from your enthusiasm about COLAs. After all, what if Mom's solution was: "Here's the same $2.50. Try to find pennies from somewhere else to get that milk!"?

Spousal Benefits

We've talked about FRA, but another big Social Security decision involves spousal benefits.

If you or your spouse has a long stretch of zeros in your earnings history — perhaps if one of you stayed home for years, caring for children or sick relatives — you may want to consider filing for spousal benefits instead of filing on your own earnings history. A spousal benefit can be up to 50 percent of the primary wage earner's benefit at full retirement age.

To begin drawing a spousal benefit, you must be at least sixty-two years old, and the primary wage earner must have already filed for their benefit. While there are penalties for taking spousal benefits early, you cannot earn credits for delaying past full retirement age.[42]

As I wrote, the spousal benefit can be a big deal for those who don't have a very long pay history, but it's important to weigh your own earned benefits against the option of withdrawing based on a fraction of your spouse's benefits.

To look at how this could play out, let's use a hypothetical couple: Mary Jane, who is sixty, and Peter, who is sixty-two.

Let's say Peter's benefit at FRA — in his case, sixty-seven — would be $1,600. If Peter begins his benefits right now (five years before FRA), his monthly check will be $1,120. If Mary Jane begins taking spousal benefits in two years at the earliest

---

[42] Social Security Administration. "Retirement Planner: Benefits For You As A Spouse" https://www.ssa.gov/planners/retire/applying6.html

date possible, her monthly benefits will be reduced to $392 per month (remember, at FRA, the most she can qualify for is half of Peter's FRA benefit).

What if Peter and Mary Jane both wait until FRA? At sixty-seven, Peter begins taking his full benefit of $1,600 a month. Two years later, when she reaches age sixty-seven, Mary Jane will qualify for $800 a month. By waiting until FRA, the couple's monthly benefit goes from $1,512 to $2,400.

What if Peter delays until age seventy to get his maximum possible benefit? For each year past FRA he delays, his monthly benefits increase by 8 percent. This means that at seventy, he could file for a monthly benefit of $1,984. However, delayed retirement credits do not affect spousal benefits, so as soon as Peter files at seventy, Mary Jane would also file (at age sixty-eight) for her maximum benefit of $800, so their highest possible combined monthly check is $2,784.[43]

When it comes to your Social Security benefits, you obviously will want to consider whether a monthly check based on a fraction of your spouse's earnings will be comparable to or larger than your own earnings history.

Divorced Spouses

There are a few considerations for those of us who have gone through a divorce. If you 1) were married for ten years or more *and* 2) have since been divorced for at least two years *and* 3) are unmarried *and* 4) your ex-spouse qualifies to begin Social Security, you qualify for a spousal benefit based on your ex-spouse's earnings history at FRA. A divorced spousal benefit is different from the married spousal benefit in one way: You

---

[43] Office of the Chief Actuary. Social Security Administration. "Social Security Benefits: Benefits for Spouses" https://www.ssa.gov/OACT/quickcalc/spouse.html#calculator

don't have to wait for your ex-spouse to file before you can file yourself.[44]

For instance, Charles and Moira were married for fifteen years before their divorce, when he was thirty-six and she was forty. Moira has been remarried for twenty years, and although Charles briefly remarried, his second marriage ended after a few years. Charles' benefits are largely calculated based on his many years of volunteering in schools, meaning his personal monthly benefit is close to zero.

Although Moira has deferred her retirement (opting to delay benefits until she is seventy), Charles can begin taking benefits calculated from Moira's work history at FRA as early as sixty-two. However, he will also have the option of waiting until FRA to collect the maximum, or 50 percent of Moira's earned monthly benefit at her FRA.

Widowed Spouses

If your marriage ended with the death of your spouse, you might claim a benefit for your spouse's earned income as their widow/widower called a survivor's benefit. Unlike spousal benefits or divorced benefits, if your spouse dies, you can claim their full benefit. Also, unlike spousal benefits, you can begin taking income when you turn sixty if you need to. However, as with other benefit options, your monthly check will be permanently reduced for withdrawing benefits before FRA.

If your spouse began taking benefits before they died, you can't delay withdrawing your survivor's benefits to get delayed credits. The Social Security Administration maintains you can only get as much from a survivor's benefit as your deceased spouse might have received had they lived.[45]

---

[44] Social Security Administration. "Retirement Planner: If You Are Divorced." https://www.ssa.gov/planners/retire/divspouse.html

[45] Social Security Administration. "Social Security Benefit Amounts For The Surviving Spouse By Year Of Birth" https://www.ssa.gov/planners/survivors/survivorchartred.html

Taxes, Taxes, Taxes

With Social Security — as with everything — it is important to consider taxes. It may be surprising, but your Social Security benefits are not tax-free. Despite having been taxed to accrue those benefits in the first place, you may have to pay Uncle Sam income taxes on up to 85 percent of your Social Security.

The Social Security Administration figures these taxes using what they call "the provisional income formula." Your provisional income formula differs from the adjusted gross income you use for your regular income taxes. Instead, to find out how much of your Social Security benefit is taxable, the Social Security Administration calculates it this way:

Provisional Income = Adjusted Gross Income + Nontaxable Interest + ½ of Social Security

See that piece about nontaxable interest? That generally means interest from government bonds and notes. It surprises many people that although you may not pay taxes on those assets, their income will count against you when it comes to Social Security taxation.

Once you have figured out your provisional income (also called "combined income"), you can use the following chart to figure out your Social Security taxes.[46]

---

[46] Social Security Administration. "Benefits Planner: Income Taxes and Your Social Security Benefits" https://www.ssa.gov/planners/taxes.html

Taxes on Social Security

Provisional Income = Adjusted Gross Income + Nontaxable Interest + ½ of Social Security

If you are ___ and your provisional income is___, then ...		Uncle Sam will tax ___ of your Social Security
Single	Married, filing jointly	
Less than $25,000	Less than $32,000	0%
$25,000 to $34,000	$32,000 to $44,000	Up to 50%
More than $34,000	More than $44,000	Up to 85%

[47]

This is one more reason why working with financial and tax professionals may benefit you. They can help you look at your entire financial picture to make your overall retirement plan as tax-efficient as possible — including your Social Security benefit.

As I noted earlier, most people take their Social Security benefits at age sixty-two when they're first eligible. Doing so could lead to a lot of money left on the table; however, depending on your situation, it could still be your best option. Let's say you retire at age sixty-two but wait until age sixty-seven to claim Social Security. In those first five years of retirement, you're taking money from your assets for income. This could be a bit of a risk because you've delayed claiming an asset that has no beneficiaries while spending down an

---

[47] Social Security Administration. 2023. "Income Taxes And Your Social Security Benefit"
https://www.ssa.gov/benefits/retirement/planner/taxes.html

investment that could be spent later or passed on to family or loved ones. Your kids don't get to spend your Social Security.

As with everything else, your decision largely depends on your situation and goals. In many cases, waiting does make sense. However, if you don't have children or your family has a history of longevity, I might suggest you go ahead and take it. I typically would not take money out of my assets when I could have otherwise taken Social Security.

Again, your choice depends on your individual situation, but this is where a good financial professional can help you determine what makes the most sense.

Working and Social Security: The Earnings Test

If you haven't reached FRA but you started your Social Security benefits and are still working, things get a little hairy.

Because you have started Social Security payments, the Social Security Administration will pay out your benefits (at that reduced rate, of course, because you haven't reached your FRA). Yet, because you are working, the organization must also withhold from your check to add to your benefits, which you are already collecting. See how this complicates matters?

To address the situation, the government has what is called the earnings test. For 2024, you can earn up to $22,320 without it affecting your Social Security check if you're younger than full retirement age. But, for every $2 you earn past that amount, the Social Security Administration will withhold $1. The earnings test loosens in the year of your FRA; if you are reaching FRA in 2024, you can earn up to $59,520 before you run into the earnings test, and the government only withholds $1 for every $3 past that amount.

The month you reach FRA, you are no longer subject to any earnings withholding. For instance, if you are still working and will turn sixty-seven on December 28, 2024, you would only have to worry about the earnings test until December, and then you can ignore it entirely. Keep in mind, the money the government withholds from your Social Security benefits while you are working before FRA will be tacked back onto your benefits check after FRA.[48]

Social Security is a big part of most people's retirement plans. For many, it's a large portion of their income, especially if they retire later. For a married couple who retires after age seventy, Social Security could represent up to $9,110 of their income per month.[49] For some, this could be enough to cover their entire expenses. I have several clients who have the means to have a higher income in retirement, but Social Security covers all their everyday expenses. In these cases, we use their assets to fund their annual vacations.

When you choose to retire and decide to take Social Security matters; it is a significant component of your retirement plan and, therefore, needs to be actively planned for taken seriously. Rules of thumb are not concrete; your situation is unique. Whether you claim Social Security early or later needs to be based on your specific situation; otherwise, you increase your chances of making a costly mistake.

Railroad Retirement Benefits

The Railroad Retirement Act was established in 1934 to address concerns about existing pension programs' ability to provide former railroad employees with old-age benefits.[50] The Act continues to provide benefits to retired and disabled workers, and their dependents, based on their length of employment in

---

[48] Social Security Administration. "Receiving Benefits While Working" https://www.ssa.gov/benefits/retirement/planner/whileworking.html
[49] Hilary Collins. SmartAsset. June 6, 2023. "Maximum Social Security Benefit for Married Couples."
https://smartasset.com/retirement/maximum-social-security-benefit-for-married-couples
[50] U.S. Railroad Retirement Board. January, 2023. "2023 Agency Overview" https://www.rrb.gov/OurAgency/AgencyOverview

the industry. Although there are similarities to Social Security, there are considerable differences, which include payment amounts, eligibility age, and taxation obligations.

Like Social Security, Railroad Retirement Benefits (RRB) are funded from payroll taxes of current employees and employers. Also, both types of benefits are received by retirees as a monthly check. RRBs use the same formula to calculate COLAs as Social Security.

The differences between the two retirement programs are intricate. The average monthly RRB payment is more generous than Social Security because railroad workers pay higher taxes into the program. Another major difference is the age at which railroad workers are eligible to begin collecting benefits: A railroad worker with thirty or more years of service is eligible for full benefits at age sixty without a reduction.

The taxation of RRBs is more complex than Social Security payments. To determine the tax, RRBs are broken down into two components:
- Tier I benefits resemble Social Security, a private pension, or a combination of both
- Tier II benefits are similar to a private pension[51]

The portion of the Tier I benefit equivalent to Social Security is taxed the same way as Social Security benefits, but the portion not equivalent is fully taxable. Regarding the Tier II, a portion is always taxable and subject to ordinary income tax rates.[52]

---

[51] Kurt Woock. Nerdwallet.com. November 30, 2023. "Railroad Retirement Board: What It Is, How It Works"
https://www.nerdwallet.com/article/investing/social-security/what-is-the-railroad-retirement-board

[52] True Tamplin. Financestrategist.com. September 7, 2023. "Is Railroad Retirement Income Taxable?"
https://www.financestrategists.com/retirement-planning/retirement-income-planning/is-railroad-retirement-income-taxable/

CHAPTER 6
401(k)s, IRAs, and Roth IRAs

Have you heard? Today's retirement is not your parents' retirement. You see, back in the day, it was pretty common to work for one company for the vast majority of your career and then retire with a gold watch and a pension.

The gold watch was a symbol of the quality time you had put in at that company, but the pension was more than a symbol. Instead, it was a guarantee — as solid as your employer — that they would repay your hard work with a certain amount of income in your old age. Did you see the caveat there? Your pension's guarantee was *as solid as your employer*. The problem was, what if your employer went under?

Companies that failed couldn't pay their retired employees' pensions, leading to financial challenges for many. Beginning in 1974 with Congress' passage of the Employee Retirement Income Security Act, federal legislation and regulations aimed at protecting retirees were everywhere. One piece of legislation included a relatively obscure section of the Internal Revenue Code, added in 1978 — Section 401(k), to be specific.

IRC section 401, subsection k, created tax advantages for employer-sponsored financial products, even if the main contributor was the employee themselves. Over the years, more employers took note, beginning an age of transition away from pensions and toward 401(k) plans. A 401(k) is a retirement account with certain tax benefits and restrictions on the investments or other financial products inside of it.

Essentially, 401(k)s and their individual retirement account (IRA) counterparts are "wrappers" that provide tax benefits around assets; typically, the assets that compose IRAs and 401(k)s are mutual funds, stock and bond mixes, and money market accounts. However, IRA and 401(k) contents are becoming more diverse these days, with some companies offering different kinds of annuity options within their plans.

Where pensions are defined-*benefit* plans, 401(k)s and IRAs are defined-*contribution* plans. The one-word change outlines the basic difference. Pensions spell out what you can expect to receive from the plan but not necessarily how much money it will take to fund those benefits. With 401(k)s, an employer sets a standard for how much they will contribute (if any), and you can be certain of what you are contributing. Still, there is no outline for what you can expect to receive in return for those contributions.

Modern employment looks very different. A 2022 survey by the Bureau of Labor Statistics determined U.S. workers stayed with their employers for a median of 4.1 years. Workers aged fifty-five to sixty-four had a little more staying power and were most likely to stay with their employer for about ten years.[53] Participation in 401(k) plans appears solid. In a study it conducted, Vanguard reported a record plan participation rate of 83 percent in 2022. Plans with automatic enrollment drew a 93 percent participation rate.[54]

Those statistics make it clear that 401(k) plans have replaced pensions at many companies and, for that matter, a gold watch.

Although pensions are now becoming the exception rather than the norm, they're still common in some industries, particularly government and civil service positions. Pensions are a great asset, especially now that interest rates have

---

[53] Bureau of Labor Statistics. September 22, 2022. "Employee Tenure Summary" https://www.bls.gov/news.release/tenure.nr0.htm
[54] Vanguard. 2023. "How America Saves 2023" https://institutional.vanguard.com/content/dam/inst/iig-transformation/has/2023/pdf/has-insights/how-america-saves-report-2023.pdf

increased. Just like Social Security and investment planning, pension planning is crucial. You want to be sure you're taking your pension in the right form. That might mean simply taking the lump sum because you have enough other investments that you don't need the income. There's a lot more that goes into pension planning than most people realize.

If there is anything to learn from this paradigm shift, it's that you must look out for yourself. Whether you have worked for a company for two years or twenty, you are still the one who has to look out for your own best interests. That holds doubly true when it comes to preparing for retirement. If you are one of the lucky ones who still has a pension, good for you. But for the rest of us, it is likely a 401(k) — or possibly one of its nonprofit- or government-sector counterparts, a 403(b) or 457 plan — is one of your biggest assets for retirement.

Some employers offer incentives to contribute to their company plans, like a company match. On that subject, I have one thing to say: *Do it!* Nothing in life is free, as they say, but a company match on your retirement funds is about as close to free money as it gets. If you can make the minimum to qualify for your company's match at all, go for it.

Now, it's likely that during our working years, we mostly "set and forget" our 401(k) funding. Because it is tax-advantaged, your employer is taking money from your paycheck — before taxes — and putting it into your plan for you. Maybe you were able to pick a selection of investments, or maybe your company only offers one choice of investment in your 401(k). Either way, while you are gainfully employed, your most impactful decision may just be the decision to continue funding your plan in the first place. But when you are ready to retire or move jobs, you have choices to make requiring a little more thought and care.

When you are ready to part ways with your job, you have a few options:
- Leave the money where it is
- Take the cash (and pay income taxes and perhaps a 10 percent additional federal tax if you are younger than age fifty-nine-and-one-half)

- Transfer the money to another employer plan (if the new plan allows)
- Roll the money over into a self-directed IRA

Now, these are just general options. You will have to decide — hopefully with the help of a financial professional — what's right for you. For instance, 401(k)s are typically pretty closely tied to the companies offering them, so when changing jobs, it may not always be possible to transfer a 401(k) to another 401(k). Leaving the money where it is may also be out of the question — some companies have direct cash payout or rollover policies once someone is no longer employed.

Also, remember what we mentioned earlier about how we change jobs more often these days? That means you likely have a 401(k) with your current company, but you may also have a string of retirement accounts trailing you from other jobs.

When you add it all up, people tend to have much more money than they think. Sometimes that's a good thing, and sometimes it's not. When people realize they have some money, suddenly they start to spend that money. It can feel like getting a big raise toward the end of your working years, leading you to create habits where you start spending more money. These habits might be small things like getting a daily Starbucks drink. This habit may be fine at first, but if you're suddenly spending $15 or $30 a day on Starbucks between you and your spouse, those purchases will add up over time—not to mention they're not great for your heart or waistline! Therefore, tracking your expenses over time is essential so you can have an accurate idea of the income you'll need once you leave the workforce behind.

When it comes to your retirement income, it's important to be able to pull together *all* your assets, so you can examine what you have and where, and then decide what you will do with it.

Tax-Qualified, Tax-Preferred, Tax-Deferred ... Still TAXED

Financial media often cite IRAs and 401(k)s for their tax benefits. After all, with traditional plans, you put your money in pre-tax, and it hopefully grows for years — even decades — untaxed. That's why these accounts are called "tax-qualified" or "tax-deferred" assets. They aren't *tax-free!* Rarely does Uncle Sam allow business to continue without receiving his piece of the pie, and your retirement assets are no different. If you didn't pay taxes on the front end, you will pay taxes on the money you withdraw from these accounts in retirement. Don't get me wrong: This isn't an inherently good or bad thing; it's just the way it is. It's important to understand, though, for the sake of planning ahead.

In retirement, many people assume they will be in a lower tax bracket. As referenced in the Taxes chapter, for retirees with healthy balances in tax-deferred assets, their retirement marginal tax rate may be the same or even more than their pre-retirement rate. The timing involved with beginning Social Security or in shifting or converting funds out of tax-deferred assets is of strategic concern because of taxes owed on those assets.

Keep in mind, IRAs, 401(k)s, and their alternatives have a few limitations because of their special tax status. For one thing, the IRS sets limits on your contributions to these retirement accounts. If you are contributing to a 401(k) or an equivalent nonprofit or government plan, your annual contribution limit is $23,000 (as of 2024). If you are fifty or older, the IRS allows additional contributions, called "catch-up contributions," of up to $7,500 on top of the regular limit of $23,000. For an IRA, the limit is $7,000, with a catch-up limit of an additional $1,000.[55] Beginning in 2026, catch-up

---

[55] Fidelity.com. November 2, 2023. "IRA contribution limits for 2022, 2023, and 2024" https://www.fidelity.com/learning-center/smart-money/ira-contribution-limits

contributions for individuals with income exceeding $145,000 must transfer into a Roth IRA.[56]

Because their tax advantages come from their intended use as retirement income, withdrawing funds from these accounts before you turn fifty-nine-and-one-half can carry stiff penalties. In addition to fees your investment management company might charge, you will have to pay income tax *and* a 10 percent federal tax penalty, with a few exceptions.

The fifty-nine-and-one-half rule for retirement accounts is incredibly important to remember, especially when you're young. Younger workers are often tempted to cash out an IRA from a previous employer and then are surprised to find their checks missing 20 percent of the account value to income taxes, penalty taxes, and account fees.

Many millennials I see in my practice say that while they may be socking money away in their workplace retirement plan, it is often the *only* place they are saving. This could be problematic later because of the fifty-nine-and-one-half rule; what if you have an emergency? It is important to fund your retirement, but you need to have some liquid assets handy as emergency funds. This can help you avoid breaking into your retirement accounts and incurring taxes and penalties because of the fifty-nine-and-one-half rule.

RMDs

Remember how we talked about the 401(k) or IRA being a "tax wrapper" for your funds? Well, eventually, Uncle Sam will want a bite of that candy bar. So, when you turn seventy-three, the government requires you to withdraw a portion of your account, which the IRS calculates based on the size of your account and your estimated lifespan. This required minimum

---

[56] Robert Powell. thestreet.com. "Ask the Hammer: Catch-up Contributions Now Permitted Until 2026"
https://www.thestreet.com/retirement-daily/ask-the-hammer/catch-up-contributions-now-permitted-until-2026

distribution (RMD) is the government's insurance it will collect some taxes from your earnings at some point. Because you didn't pay taxes on the front end, you will now pay income taxes on whatever you withdraw — including your RMDs.

Let me reiterate something I pointed out in the Longevity chapter. Beginning at age seventy-three, you are required to withdraw a certain minimum amount every year from your 401(k) or IRA, or else you will face a tax penalty on any RMD monies you should have withdrawn but didn't — and that's on top of income tax. The SECURE Act 2.0 reduced the penalty to 25 percent (from 50 percent). Timely corrections also can reduce the penalty to 10 percent.[57]

Even after you begin RMDs, you can still continue contributing to your 401(k) or IRAs if you are still employed, which can affect the whole discussion on RMDs and possible tax considerations. The SECURE Act 2.0 raised the RMD age to seventy-three from seventy-two. In addition, the latest legislation stipulates the RMD age will increase to seventy-five for those turning seventy-four after December 31, 2032.[58]

If you don't need income from your retirement accounts, RMDs can seem like more of a tax burden than an income boon. While some people prefer to reinvest their RMDs, this comes with the possibility of additional taxation: You'll pay income taxes on your RMDs and then potential capital gains taxes on the growth of your investments. If you are legacy-minded, there are other ways to use RMDs, many of which have tax benefits.

SECURE 2.0 Act provisions

In addition to changes imposed for RMD ages, Secure Act 2.0 also expanded access to retirement savings using different methods. Provisions in the legislation go into effect at different times, ranging from 2023-25.

---

[57] Jim Probasco. Investopedia.com. January 6, 2023. "SECURE 2.0 Act of 2022" https://www.investopedia.com/secure-2-0-definition-5225115
[58] Ibid.

- Beginning January 2, 2024, plan participants can access up to $1,000 (once a year) from retirement savings for emergency, personal, or family expenses without paying a 10 percent early-withdrawal penalty.
- Beginning January 2, 2024, employees can establish a Roth emergency savings account of up to $2,500 per participant.
- Beginning January 2, 2024, domestic abuse survivors can withdraw the lesser of $10,000 or 50 percent of their retirement account without penalty.[59]
- Beginning January 1, 2023, victims of a qualified, federally declared disaster can withdraw up to $22,000 from their retirement account without penalty.[60]

Permanent Life Insurance

One way to turn those pesky RMDs into a legacy is through permanent life insurance. Assuming you need the death benefit coverage and can qualify for it medically, if properly structured, these products can pass on a sizeable death benefit to your beneficiaries — tax-free — as part of your general legacy plan.

ILIT

Another way to use RMDs toward your legacy is to work with an estate planning attorney to create an irrevocable life insurance trust (ILIT). This is basically a permanent life insurance policy placed within a trust. Because the trust is irrevocable, you would relinquish control of it, but unlike with just a permanent life insurance policy, your death benefit won't count toward your taxable estate.

---

[59] Betterment.com. January 12, 2023. "SECURE Act 2.0: Signed into Law" https://www.betterment.com/work/resources/secure-act-2

[60] Charlie Pastor. Motley Fool. February 16, 2023. "Law Opens New Doors for Penalty-Free Retirement Account Distributions" www.fool.com/the-ascent/buying-stocks/articles/law-opens-new-doors-for-penalty-free-retirement-account-distributions.

Annuities

Because annuities can be tax-deferred, using all or a portion of your RMDs to fund an annuity contract can be one way to further delay taxation while guaranteeing your income payments (either to you or your loved ones) later. Of course, this assumes you don't need the RMD income during your retirement.

Qualified Charitable Distributions

If you are charity-minded, you may use your RMDs toward a charitable organization instead of using them for income. You must do this directly from your retirement account (you can't take the RMD check and *then* pay the charity) for your withdrawals to be qualified charitable distributions (QCDs), but this is one way of realizing some of the benefits of a charitable legacy during your own lifetime. You will not need to pay taxes on your QCDs, and they won't count toward your annual charitable tax deduction limit, plus you'll be able to see how the organization you are supporting uses your donations. You should consult a financial professional on how to correctly make a QCD.

Spend Early

Another strategy for mitigating RMDs is to spend some of your tax-deferred dollars earlier in retirement. In other words, we don't want all those tax-deferred dollars to grow, grow, grow because that means your tax bill will grow, grow, grow as well. Using some of that tax-deferred money early on rather than other income that might have more tax advantages can help reduce your tax bill over time. Using a strategy like a Roth conversion ahead of time can potentially reduce your tax burden as well.

With tax strategies, a lot of planning comes down to understanding how the tax code works and trying to get ahead of it. Still, we all know the saying: death and taxes are the only things guaranteed in life.

Roth IRA

Since the Taxpayer Relief Act of 1997, there has been a different kind of retirement account — or "tax wrapper" — available to the public: the Roth. Roth IRAs and Roth 401(k)s each differ from their traditional counterparts in one big way: You pay your taxes on the front end. Once your post-tax money is in the Roth account, as long as you follow the rules and limitations of that account, your distributions are truly tax-free. You won't pay income tax when you take withdrawals, so in turn, you don't have to worry about RMDs. However, Roth accounts have the same limitations as traditional 401(k)s and IRAs when it comes to withdrawing money before age fifty-nine-and-one-half, with the added stipulation that the account must have been open for at least five years for the account holder to make withdrawals.

Taking Charge

As mentioned earlier, the 401(k) and IRA have largely replaced pensions, but they aren't an equal trade.

Pensions are employer-funded; the money feeding into them is money that wouldn't ever show up on your pay stub. Because 401(k)s are self-funded, you must actively and consciously save. This distinction has made a difference when it comes to funding retirement. Fidelity Investments published a study detailing the average 401(k) balance for a person aged fifty-five to sixty-four is $189,800, but the median likely tells the full story. The median 401(k) balance for a person aged fifty-five to sixty-four is $56,450. Those figures reflect Fidelity accounts from the third quarter of 2022.[61]

There can be many reasons why people underfund their retirement plans, like being overwhelmed by investment choices or taking withdrawals from IRAs when they leave an employer. Still, the reason at the top of the list seems to be this: People simply aren't participating to begin with.

So, whether you use a 401(k) with an employer or an IRA alternative with a private company separate from your workplace, the most important retirement savings decision you can make is to sock away your money somewhere in the first place.

---

[61] Arielle O'Shea. Nerd Wallet. December 22, 2022. "The Average 401(k) Balance by Age" https://www.nerdwallet.com/article/investing/the-average-401k-balance-by-age

CHAPTER 7

Annuities

In my practice, I offer my clients a variety of products — from securities to insurance —designed to help them work toward their financial goals. You may be wondering: Why single out a single product in this book?

Well, while most of my clients have a pretty good understanding of business and finance, I sometimes find those who have the impression magic must be involved. Some people assume there is a magic finance wand we can wave to change years' worth of savings into a strategy for retirement income. But it's not as easy as a goose laying golden eggs or the Fairy Godmother turning a pumpkin into a coach!

Finances aren't magic; it takes lots of hard work and, typically, several financial products and strategies to pull together a complete retirement plan. Of all the financial products I work with, it seems people find none more mysterious than annuities. And, if I may say, even some of those who recognize the word "annuity" have a limited understanding of the product. So, in the interest of demystifying annuities, let me tell you a little about what an annuity is.

In general, insurance is a financial hedge against risk. Car owners buy auto insurance to protect their finances in case they injure someone or someone injures them. Homeowners have house insurance to protect their assets in case of a fire, flood, or another disaster. People have life insurance to help protect their finances in case of untimely death. Almost juxtaposed to life insurance, people have annuities in case of a long life;

annuities can give you financial confidence by providing consistent and reliable income payments.

The basic premise of an annuity is you, the annuitant, pay an insurance company some amount in exchange for their contractual guarantee they will pay you income for a certain time period. How that company pays you, for how long, and how much they offer are all determined by the annuity contract you enter into with the insurance company.

The Ways You Get Paid

There are several ways for an annuity contract to provide income: annuitization, income riders, partial surrenders, and settlement options for heirs.

Annuitization

When someone "annuitizes" a contract, it is the point where they turn on the income stream. Once a contract has been annuitized, there is no going back. With annuities, if the policyholder lives longer than the insurance company planned, the insurance company is still obligated to pay them, even if the payments end up being way more than the contract's actual value.

If, however, the policyholder dies an untimely death, depending on the contract type, the insurance company may keep anything left of the money that funded the annuity. Nothing would be paid out to the contract holder's survivors. You see where that could make some people balk? Now, modern annuities rarely rely on annuitization for the income portion of the contract, and instead have so many bells and whistles that the old concept of annuitization seems outdated, but because this is still an option, it's important to at least understand the basic concept.

Riders

Speaking of bells and whistles, let's talk about riders. Modern annuities have a lot of different options these days, many in the form of riders you can add to your contract for a fee. The fee typically amounts to 1 percent of the contract value per year. Each rider has its particulars, and the types of riders available will vary by the type of annuity contract purchased, but I'll just briefly outline some of these little extras:

- Lifetime income rider: Contract guarantees you an enhanced or flexible income for life
- Death benefit rider: Contract pays an enhanced death benefit to your beneficiaries, even if you have annuitized
- Return of premium rider: Guarantees you (or your beneficiaries) will at least receive back the premium value of the annuity
- Long-term care rider: Provides a certain amount, sometimes as much as twice the normal income benefit amount for a period of time to help pay for long-term care if the contract holder is moved to a nursing home or assisted living situation

This isn't an extensive look, and usually the riders have fancier names based on the issuing company, like "Lorem Ipsum Insurance Company Income Preferred Bonus Fixed Index Annuity rider," but I just wanted to show you what some of the general options are in layperson's terms.

Partial Surrender

Most annuities offer a free withdrawal provision that is often referred to as a partial surrender. An annuity contract typically allows for an annual withdrawal of up to 10 percent, typically, of the account value or of the premium originally paid. The option to make this withdrawal, typically without penalty, can be used as a tool to help with your income planning strategies.

Keep in mind, the withdrawal is subject to income taxes, and an additional 10 percent IRS penalty if you're under age fifty-nine-and-one-half.

This percentage can be accessed during the surrender period and can be a sound strategy, especially for a client who does not require a regular influx of income provided by a rider. After the surrender value period, the holder of the annuity can access the annuity without losing control of the account value.

I find the partial surrender strategy to often be effective for my clients, particularly if they do not need regular income generated through the use of a rider. A partial surrender allows for the annuity holder to just take out funds when a need arises.

Settlement Options

While any value of an annuity left to beneficiaries upon the annuity holder's death is fairly self-explanatory, there is a point worth raising. Heirs have different settlement options they can consider, including opportunities for lump sums, periodic payments, or specific payouts.

Specific payouts are often based on tax considerations involving a beneficiary or multiple beneficiaries. As an advanced tax planning measure, I have clients who have addressed tax implications with their heirs regarding the most advantageous method for arranging a settlement option that eases any tax burden on the beneficiary.

Types of Annuities

Annuities break down into four basic types: immediate, variable, fixed, and fixed index.

Immediate

Immediate annuities primarily rely on annuitization to provide income. You give the insurance company a lump sum up front, and your payments begin immediately. Once you begin receiving income payments, the transaction is irreversible, and you no longer have access to your money in a lump sum. When you die, any remaining contract value is typically forfeited to the insurance company.

All other annuity contract types are "deferred" contracts, meaning you fund your policy as a lump sum or over a period of years. You give it the opportunity to grow over time — sometimes years, sometimes decades.

Variable

A variable annuity is an insurance contract as well as a security product. It's sold by insurance companies, but only through someone who is also registered to sell securities products. With a variable annuity contract, the insurance company invests your premiums in sub-accounts that are tied to the stock market.

This makes it a bit different from the other annuity contract types because it is the only contract where your money is subject to losses because of market declines. Your contract value has a greater opportunity to grow, but it also stands to lose. Additionally, your contract's value will be subject to the underlying investment's fees and limitations — including capital gains taxes, management fees, etc. Once it is time for you to receive income from the contract, the insurance company will pay you a certain income, locked in at whatever your contract's value was.

Fixed

A traditional fixed annuity is pretty straightforward. You purchase a contract with a guaranteed interest rate, and when you are ready, the insurance company will make regular income payments to you at whatever payout rate your contract guarantees. Those payments will continue for the rest of your life and, if you choose, for the remainder of your spouse's life.

Fixed annuities don't typically offer significant upside potential, but many people like them for their guarantees and predictability. After all, if your Aunt May lives to be ninety-five, knowing she has a paycheck later in life can be her mental and financial safety net. Unlike variable annuities, which are subject to market risk and might be up one year and down the next, you can easily calculate the value of your fixed annuity over your lifetime.

Fixed Index

To recap, variable annuities take on more risk to offer more possibilities to grow. Fixed annuities have less potential growth, but they protect your principal. In the last couple of decades, many insurance companies have retooled their product line to offer fixed indexed annuities (FIAs), which are sort of midway between variable and fixed annuities on that risk/reward spectrum. Fixed index annuities offer greater growth potential than traditional fixed annuities but less than variable annuities. Like traditional fixed annuities, however, fixed index annuities are protected from downside market losses.

Fixed index annuities earn interest that is tied to an external market index, meaning that instead of your contract value growing at a set interest rate like a traditional fixed annuity, it has the potential to grow within a range. Your contract's value is credited interest based on the performance of an external market index like the S&P 500® while never being invested in the market itself. You can't invest in the S&P 500® directly, but depending on when your contract credits interest to your account, your annuity has the potential to earn interest based on the chosen index's performance, subject to limits set by the company (such as caps, spreads, and participation rates).

For instance, if your contract caps your interest at 5 percent, then in a year that the S&P 500® gains 3 percent, your annuity value increases 3 percent. If the S&P 500® gains 35 percent, your annuity value gets a 5 percent interest bump. But since your money isn't actually invested in the market with a fixed index annuity, if the market nosedives (such as happened during 2000, 2008, 2020, and 2022, anyone?), you won't see any increase in your contract value. Conversely, there will also be no decrease in your contract value, no matter how badly the market performs. As long as you follow the terms of the contract, you won't lose any of the interest you were credited in previous years.

So, what if the S&P 500® shows a market loss of 30 percent? Your contract value isn't going anywhere unless you purchased an optional rider. This charge will still come out of your annuity value each year, along with possible mortality, expense, and administrative fees. For those who are more interested in protection than significant growth potential, fixed index annuities can be an attractive option. When the stock market has a long period of positive performance, a fixed index annuity can enjoy conservative growth. And during stretches where the stock market is erratic and stock values across the board take significant losses? Fixed index annuities won't lose anything due to the stock market volatility.

Like anything else, FIAs are a tool to be used when it makes sense. I like using them for income guarantees or their conservative growth potential. With an FIA, your account value doesn't necessarily go up and down with interest rates, so, as previously noted, they don't have the same rate of risk as other products. However, they do come with the caveat of needing to be held until term, and growth is not guaranteed.

Annuities have gotten a bad name over the years, usually because people don't understand the different types and end up with the wrong product for their situation. Those experiences don't make annuities a bad tool; it just means these individuals had the wrong brand of tool. Think of it like this: You use a hammer for nails and a screwdriver for screws. When I see people upset about their annuity product, it is usually because they're trying to hammer in a screw or screw in a nail. In other words, maybe they didn't need retirement income, but they have an income-based product. Or they need income but don't have any income-based products, so their product's withdrawal fees quickly eat away at its value. With any tool, you must evaluate if it's the ideal for the job or if there is something more appropriate you should be using; FIAs are no different.

Other Things to Know About Annuities

We just explained the four kinds of annuity contracts available, but all of them have some commonalities as annuities.

For all annuities, the contractual guarantees are only as strong as the insurance company that sells the product, which makes it important to thoroughly check the credit ratings of any company whose products you are considering.

Annuities are tax-deferred, meaning you don't have to pay taxes on interest earnings each year as the contract value grows. Instead, you will pay ordinary income taxes on your withdrawals. These are meant to be long-term products, so like other tax-deferred or tax-advantaged products, if you begin taking withdrawals from your contract before age fifty-nine-and-one-half, you may also have to pay a 10 percent federal tax penalty. Also, while annuities are generally considered illiquid, some contracts allow you to withdraw up to 10 percent of your contract value every year. Withdraw any more, however, and you could incur additional surrender penalties.

Keep in mind, your withdrawals will deplete the accumulated cash value, death benefit, and possibly the rider values of your contract.

Annuities aren't for everyone, but it's important to understand them before saying "yea" or "nay" on whether they fit into your plan; otherwise, you're not operating with complete information, wouldn't you agree? Regardless, you should talk to a financial professional who can help you understand annuities, dissect your particular financial needs, and show you whether an annuity is appropriate for your retirement income plan.

CHAPTER 8

Estate & Legacy

In my practice, I devote a significant portion of my time to matters of estates. That doesn't mean drawing up wills or trusts or putting together powers of attorney or anything like that. After all, I'm not an estate planning attorney. But I am a financial professional, and what part of the "estate" isn't affected by money matters?

I've included this chapter because I have seen many people do estate planning wrong. Clients, or clients' families, have come in after experiencing a death in the family and have found themselves in the middle of probate, high taxes, or a discovery of something unforeseen (often long-term care) draining the estate.

I have also seen people do estate planning right: clients or families who visit my office to talk about legacies and ways to make them last, and adult children who have room to grieve without an added burden of unintended costs or stress from a family devastated because of inadequate planning.

I'll share some of these stories here. However, I'm not going to give you specific advice, since everyone's situation is unique. I only want to give you some things to think about and to underscore the importance of planning ahead.

As I noted, I'm not an estate planning attorney, but I work with several—some of whom even come into my office to meet with clients. Consulting with these specialists is essential because attorneys often bring a different viewpoint than financial advisors. For example, there may be legal reasons for arranging for particular beneficiaries, which directly contrast with financial reasons for opposite arrangements. Having a strategic relationship with an attorney who does estate work for our clients means we can discuss potentially conflicting or complicated legal and financial elements to recommend strategies that help our clients pursue their financial goals.

There was a couple who had an old estate plan with language that didn't fit the language requirements for the state of Michigan. Essentially, they had paid a lot of money to an attorney who wasn't looking at things from a holistic financial perspective. The clients ended up with a trust that was improperly set up. If one spouse died, half of their assets became completely irrevocable, meaning the remaining spouse could not change or adjust those assets to fit their new situation, all because of the improper language included in the trust setup. Luckily, they were able to rectify the problem with the help of one of our estate attorneys. They redid the trust, included the correct language and setup for the beneficiaries, and saved a lot of potential headaches down the line.*

You Can't Take It With You

When it comes to legacy and estate, the most important thing is to *do it*. I have heard people from clients to celebrities (rap artist Snoop Dogg comes to mind) say they aren't interested in what happens to their assets when they die because they'll be dead. That's certainly one way to look at it. But I think that's a very selfish way to go about things. We all have people and causes we care about, and those who care about us. Even if the people we love don't *need* what we leave behind, they can still be fined or legally tied up in the probate process or burial costs if we don't plan for those. And that's not even considering what happens if you become incapacitated at some point while you

---

* This is a hypothetical example provided for illustrative purposes only; it does not represent a real life scenario, and should not be construed as advice designed to meet the particular needs of an individual's situation.

are still alive. Having a plan in place can greatly help reduce the stress of those responsibilities on your loved ones; it's just a loving thing to do.

Documents

There are a few documents that lay the groundwork of legacy planning. You've probably heard of all or most of them, but I'd like to review what they are and how people commonly use them. These are all things you should talk about with an estate planning attorney to establish your legacy.

Powers of Attorney

A power of attorney, or POA, is a document giving someone the authority to act on your behalf and in your best interests. These come in handy in situations where you cannot be present (think of a vacation where you get stuck in Canada), or for durable powers of attorney (DPOA), even when you are incapacitated (think in a coma or coping with dementia).

It is important to have powers of attorney in place and to appoint someone you trust to act on your behalf in these matters. Have you ever heard of someone who was incapacitated after a car accident, whether from head trauma or being in a coma for weeks — sometimes months? Do you think their bills stopped coming due during that time? I like my phone company and my bank, but neither one is about to put a moratorium on sending me bills — particularly not for an extended or interminable period. A power of attorney would have the authority to pay your mortgage or cancel your cable while you are unable.

You can have multiple attorneys-in-fact and require them to act jointly.
What this looks like: Do you think two heads are better than one? One man, Chris, significantly relied on his two sons'

opinions for both his business and personal matters. He appointed both sons as attorneys-in-fact, requiring both their signoffs for his medical and financial matters.

You can have multiple attorneys-in-fact who can act independently.

What this looks like: Irene had three children with whom she routinely stayed. They lived in different areas of the country, which she thought was an advantage; one month she might be hiking out West, the next she could enjoy the newest off-Broadway production, and the next she could soak up some Southern sun. She named her three children as independently authorized attorneys-in-fact, so if something happened, no matter where she was, the child closest could step in to act on her behalf.

You can have attorneys-in-fact who have different responsibilities.

What this looks like: Although Luke's friend Claire, a nurse, was his go-to and attorney-in-fact for health-related issues, financial matters usually made her nervous, so he appointed his good neighbor, Matt, as his attorney-in-fact in all of his financial and legal matters.

In addition to POAs, it may be helpful to have an advanced health care directive. This is a document where you have pre-decided what choices you would make about different health scenarios. An advanced health care directive can help ease the burden for your medical attorney-in-fact and loved ones, particularly when it comes to end-of-life care.

Wills

Perhaps the most basic document of legacy planning, a will is a legal document wherein you outline your wishes for your estate. When it comes to your estate after your death, having a will is the foundation of your legacy. Without one, your loved ones are left behind to guess what you would have wanted, and the court will likely split your assets according to the state's probate laws. As far as anyone knows, maybe that's exactly what you wanted, right? Because even if you told your nephew he could have your car he's been driving, if it's not in writing, it still might go to the brother, sister, son, or daughter to whom you aren't speaking.

However, it may not be enough just to have a will. Even with a will, your assets will be subject to probate. Probate is what we call the state's process for determining a will's validity. A judge will go through your will to question if it conflicts with state law, if it is the most up-to-date document, if you were mentally competent at the time it was in order, etc. For some, this is a quick, easily resolved process. For others particularly if someone steps forward to contest the will, it may take years to settle, all the while subjecting the assets to court costs and attorney's fees.

One other undesirable piece of the probate process is that it is a public process. That means anyone can go to the courthouse, ask for copies of the case, and discover your assets. They can also see who is slated to receive what and who is disputing.

A good example of how destructive probate can be seen directly in the case of Aretha Franklin, legendary "Queen of Soul" who died in 2018 with an estate valued at around $18 million. At the time of her passing, Franklin had no estate plan and two separate wills. One will, dated 2010, was found in an old cabinet in her home and favored her son, Ted White Jr. The second, a four-page handwritten document dated 2014, was found in a couch cushion and favored her son, Kecalf. While the 2014 will was eventually declared the rightful legal will, her children spent five years locked in a legal battle that exposed many details of the notoriously private singer's personal life to the public—something Franklin would no doubt not have wanted. This situation could have been avoided had a proper estate plan been set up before the singer's death.[62]

It's also important to remember beneficiary designations trump wills. So, that large life insurance policy? What if, when you bought it fifteen years ago, you wrote your ex-husband's name on the beneficiary line? Even if you stipulate otherwise in your will, the company that holds your policy will pay out to your ex-spouse. Or how about the thousands of dollars in your IRA you dedicated to the children thirty years ago, but one of your children was killed in a car accident, leaving his wife and two toddlers behind? That IRA is going to transfer to your remaining children, with nothing for your daughter-in-law and grandchildren.

That may paint a grim portrait, but I can't underscore enough the importance of working with a skilled estate planning attorney to keep your will and beneficiary designations up to date as your life changes.

Trusts

Another piece of legacy planning to consider is the trust.

A trust is set up through an estate-planning attorney who appoints and authorizes a third party, or trustee, to administer the trust (e.g., make decisions, manage the assets in the trust, distribute funds from the trust, etc.) according to the provisions of the trust agreement.

Many people are skeptical of trusts because they assume trusts are only appropriate for the fabulously wealthy. A simple trust will likely cost more than $1,000 if prepared by an estate-planning attorney, and fees can be higher for couples.[63] But a

---

[62] Ryan Patrick Hooper. NPR. July 12, 2023. "Jury rules handwritten will found under Aretha Franklin's couch cushion is valid." https://www.npr.org/2023/07/12/1187175707/jury-rules-handwritten-will-found-under-aretha-franklins-couch-cushion-is-valid

[63] Rickie Houston. smartasset.com. August 31, 2022. "How Much Does It Cost to Set Up a Trust? https://smartasset.com/estate-planning/how-much-does-it-cost-to-set-up-a-trust

trust can help you avoid both the expense and publicity of probate, provide a more immediate transfer of wealth, avoid some taxes, and provide you greater control over your legacy.

For instance, if you want to set aside some funds for a grandchild's college education, you can make it a requirement that they enroll in classes before your trust will dispense any funds. Like a will, beneficiary designations will override your trust conditions, so you must still keep your beneficiary designations on things like insurance policies and other assets up to date.

Like any financial or legal consideration, there are many options these days beyond the simple "yes or no" question of whether to have a trust. For one thing, you will need to consider if you want your trust to be revocable (you can change the terms while you are alive) or irrevocable (can't be changed; you are no longer the "owner" of the contents).

A brief note here about irrevocable trusts: Although they have significant and greater tax benefits, they are still subject to a Medicaid look-back period. If you transfer your assets into an irrevocable trust in an attempt to shelter them from a Medicaid spend-down, you will be ineligible for Medicaid coverage of long-term care for five years. However, an irrevocable trust can avoid both probate and estate taxes, and it can even help protect assets from legal judgments against you.

Another thing to remember when it comes to trusts, in general, is that even if you have set up a trust, you must remember to fund it. In my many years in this industry, I've had numerous clients come to me assuming they have helped protect their assets with a trust. When we talk about taxes and other pieces of their legacy, it turns out they never retitled any assets or changed any paperwork on the assets they wanted in the trust. So, please remember, a trust is just a bunch of fancy legal papers if you haven't followed through on retitling your assets.

Taxes

Although charitable contributions, trusts, and other tax-efficient strategies can reduce your tax bill, it's unlikely your estate will be passed on entirely tax-free. Yet, when it comes to building a legacy that can last for generations, taxes can be one of the heaviest drains on the impact of your hard work.

For 2024, the federal estate exemption was $13.61 million per individual and $27.22 million for a married couple, with estates facing up to a 40 percent tax rate after that.[64] Currently, the new estate limits are set to increase with inflation until January 1, 2026, when they will "sunset" back to the inflation-adjusted 2017 limits.[65] And that's not taking into account the various state regulations and taxes regarding estate and inheritance transfers.

Another tax concern "frequent flyer": retirement accounts.

Your IRA or 401(k) can be a source of tax issues when you pass away. For one thing, taking funds from a sizeable account can trigger a large tax bill. However, if you leave the assets in the account, there are still required minimum distributions (RMDs), which will take effect even after you die. If you pass the account to your spouse, they can keep taking your RMDs as is, or your spouse can retitle the account in their name and receive RMDs based on their life expectancy. Remember, if you don't take your RMDs, the IRS will take up to 25 percent of your required distribution (10 percent if corrections are made in a timely fashion). You will still have to pay income taxes whenever you withdraw that money. Provisions in the original SECURE Act require anyone who inherits your IRA, with few exceptions (your spouse, a beneficiary less than ten years

---

[64] Kiplinger.com. Katelyn Washington. November 15, 2023. "Estate Tax Exemption Amount Increases for 2024"
https://www.kiplinger.com/taxes/estate-tax-exemption-amount-increases
[65] IRS.gov. December 20, 2022. "What's New — Estate and Gift Tax"
https://www.irs.gov/businesses/small-businesses-self-employed/whats-new-estate-and-gift-tax

younger, or a disabled adult child, to name a few), will need to empty the account within ten years of your death.

Also — and this is a pretty big also — check with an estate-planning attorney if you are considering putting your IRA or 401(k) in a trust. An improperly titled beneficiary form for the IRA could mean the difference of thousands of dollars in taxes. This is just one more reason to work with a financial professional, one who can strategically partner with an estate planning attorney and also a tax advisory to diligently check your decisions.

CHAPTER 9

Women Retire Too

I help men, women, and families from all walks of life on their journey to and through retirement. However, we want to address the female demographic specifically. Why? It's possible that women must contend with potentially more hardship in retirement than men.

The overall poverty rate for women slightly exceeds the rate for men, but among those seventy-five years and older, 13.51 percent of women live at the poverty rate compared to 8.82 percent of men.[66]

The topics, products, and strategies I cover elsewhere in this book are meant to help address retirement concerns for men *and* women, but the dire statistic above is a reminder that much of traditional planning is geared toward men. Male careers, male lifespans, male health care. The bottom line is women's career paths often look much different than men's, so why would their retirement planning look the same?

Women often embrace different roles and values than men as workers, wives, mothers, and daughters. They are more apt to take on roles as caretakers, thus women are likely to spend portions of their lives making hard shifts between family and careers. Time out of the workforce means less income accumulation for investments and retirement. Also, non-

---

[66] statistica.com. 2023. "Poverty rate in the United States in 2021, by age and gender" https://www.statista.com/statistics/233154/us-poverty-rate-by-gender/

working years count as zeroes when calculating Social Security benefits. Women who strongly value family and community tend to focus on lifetime gifting and legacy funding, sometimes to the detriment of their own lifestyles.

These unique choices, challenges, and hurdles make a solid case that women deserve special consideration from financial professionals. The argument is further promoted by the fact that 69 percent of men in the U.S. age sixty-five and older happen to be married, compared to 47 percent of women in that age classification.[67] Single women don't have the opportunity to capitalize on the resource pooling and potential economies of scale accompanying a marriage or partnership.

In general, women need to become more involved in their current and future finances. Traditionally, men have more often been in charge of a couple's finances. But what happens if the husband passes away first (which is statistically likely, as we've shown) and the wife has been left entirely in the dark about their finances? These situations can add considerable hardship for women when they're already dealing with the emotional devastation of losing their spouse.

Women need to be a part of their financial planning. That's why we insist that both spouses be present during our first meetings with new clients. If you come in without your spouse, 99 percent of the time, we'll tell you to come back when your spouse is with you because both parties need to be equally informed. Both spouses must be involved in the second most important aspect of their life outside their health (not including families, religion, etc.).

Be Informed

With all the couples I've seen, there is almost always an "alpha" when it comes to finances. It isn't always men. For many of my

---

[67] Administration for Community Living. November 30, 2022. "Profile of Older Americans" https://acl.gov/aging-and-disability-in-america/data-and-research/profile-older-americans

coupled clients, the wife is the alpha who keeps the books and budgets and knows where all of the family's assets are, down to the penny. Yet, statistically, among baby boomers, it is usually a man who runs the books. But as time goes on, it looks like the ratio of male to female financial alphas is evening out, based on my experience speaking with couples.

Because most of the baby boomer alphas are men, there is an all too familiar scene in many financial offices across the country: A woman comes into an appointment carrying a sack full of unopened envelopes. Often through tears, she sits across the desk from a financial professional and apologizes her way through a conversation about what financial products she owns and where her income is coming from. She is recently widowed and was sure her spouse was taking care of the finances, but now she doesn't know where all their assets are kept, and her confidence in her financial outlook has wavered after walking through funeral expenses and realizing she's down to one income.

Often, she may be financially "okay." Yet, the uncertainty can be wearying, particularly when the family is already reeling from a loss. While this scenario sometimes plays out with men, in my experience, it's more likely to be a woman in that chair across from my desk. Although the practice has been leveling more and more in recent decades, for centuries Western traditions held money management down as being "a guy thing." But it doesn't have to be this way. This all-too-common scenario can be wiped away with just a little preparation.

Talk to Your Spouse/ Work with a Financial Professional

While there are many factors affecting women's financial preparation for and situation in retirement, I cannot emphasize enough that the decision to be informed, to be a part of the conversation, and to be aware of what is going on with your finances is absolutely paramount to a confident retirement.

The breakdown regarding couples and finances seems to happen because of a lack of communication The breakdown often seems to stem from no one other than the financial alpha knowing how much the family has and where. In the end, it doesn't matter who handles the money; it's about all parties being informed of what's going on financially.

There are a lot of ways to open the conversation about money. One woman, Ann, started a conversation with her husband, the financial alpha, by sitting down and saying, "Teach me how to be a widow." Perhaps that sounds grim, but it was to the point, and it spurred what she said was a very fruitful conversation. Couples sometimes have their first real conversation about money, assets, and their retirement income approach in our office. The important thing about having these conversations isn't where, it's when. The best "when" is as soon as possible.

Ann told me that after they got the conversation rolling, she and her husband spent a day — just one part of an otherwise dull weekend — going through everything she might need to know. They spent the better part of two decades together after that. When he died and she was widowed, she said the "widowhood" talk had made a huge difference. She knew who to call to talk through their retirement plan and where to call for the insurance policy.

She said the benefit of the weekend exercise they engaged in some twenty years earlier couldn't have been more apparent than when she ultimately accompanied a recently widowed friend to a financial appointment. Her friend was emotional the whole time, afraid she would run out of money any day. The financial professional ultimately showed the friend that she was financially in good shape, but not before the friend had already spent months worried that each check would exhaust her bank account. That's no way to live after losing a loved one. It was preventable had her deceased spouse and financial professional included her in a conversation about "widowhood."

Spouse-Specific Options

One area where it might be especially important to be on the same page between spouses is when it comes to financial products or services that have spousal options. A few that come to mind are pensions and Social Security, although life insurance and annuity policies also have the potential to affect both spouses.

With pensions, taking the worker's life-only option is somewhat attractive. After all, the monthly payment is bigger. However, you and your spouse should discuss your options. When we're talking about both of you as opposed to just one lifespan, there is an increased likelihood at least one of you will live a long, long time. This means the monthly payout will be less, but it also could help ensure that no matter which spouse outlives the other, no one will have to suffer the loss of a needed pension paycheck in their later retirement years.

While we covered Social Security options in a different chapter, I think some of the spousal information bears repeating. Particularly, if you worked exclusively inside the home for a significant number of years, you may want to talk about taking your Social Security benefits based on your spouse's work history. After all, Social Security is based on your thirty-five highest-earning years.

Things to remember about the spousal benefits:[68]
- Your benefit will be calculated as a percentage (up to 50 percent) of your spouse's earned monthly benefit at their full retirement age (or FRA).
- For you to begin receiving a spousal benefit, your spouse must have already filed for their benefits, and you must be at least sixty-two.
- You can qualify for a full half of your spouse's benefits if you wait until you reach FRA to file.

---

[68] Social Security Administration. "Retirement Planner: Benefits For You As A Spouse" https://www.ssa.gov/planners/retire/applying6.html

- Beginning your benefits earlier than your FRA will reduce your monthly check, but waiting to file until after FRA will not increase your benefits.

For divorcees:[69]
- You may qualify for an ex-spousal benefit if ...
    a. You were married for a decade or more
    b. **and** you are at least sixty-two
    c. **and** you have been divorced for at least two years
    d. **and** you are currently unmarried
    e. **and** your ex-spouse is sixty-two (qualifies to begin taking Social Security)
- Your ex-spouse does not need to have filed for you to file on their benefit.
- Similar to spousal benefits, you can qualify for up to half of your ex-spouse's benefits if you wait to file until your FRA.
- If your ex-spouse dies, you may file to receive a widow/widower benefit on their Social Security record as long as you are at least age sixty and fulfill all the other requirements on the preceding alphabetized list.
    a. This will not affect the benefits of your ex-spouse's current spouse

For widow's (or widower's, for that matter) benefits:[70]
- You may qualify to receive as much as your deceased spouse would have received if ...
    a. You were married for at least nine months before their death

---

[69] Social Security Administration. "Retirement Planner: If You Are Divorced" https://www.ssa.gov/planners/retire/divspouse.html
[70] Social Security Administration. "Survivors Planner: If You Are The Worker's Widow Or Widower" https://www.ssa.gov/planners/survivors/ifyou.html#h2

b. *or* you would qualify for a divorced spousal benefit (if you were divorced and your ex-spouse dies)
   c. *and* you are at least sixty
   d. *and* you did not/have not remarried before age sixty
- You may earn delayed credits on your spouse's benefit *if* your spouse hadn't already filed for benefits when they died.
- Other rules may apply to you if you are disabled or are caring for a deceased spouse's dependent or disabled child.

Longevity

On average, women live longer than men. Most stats put average female longevity at about two years more than men. But averages are tricky things. An April 2022 report by the World Economic Forum listed the eight oldest people in the world to all be women. They ranged in age from 114 years old to 118 and included two Americans.[71]

It's an exciting time to be a woman, as their potential life paths are vast and less subject to judgment than probably at any point in history. Want to stay at home and raise children? Wonderful! Get a PhD in Astrophysics and work for NASA? Fantastic! Do a combination of both? It's happening! On one hand, women all have unique personalities, goals, ambitions, and passions. However, they share biological and instinctual traits that, in general, give rise to longer lives. And, on that note, the trend for women to live longer presents longstanding financial ramifications.

---

[71] Martin Armstrong. World Economic Forum. April 29, 2022. "How old are the world's oldest people?"
https://www.weforum.org/agenda/2022/04/the-oldest-people-in-the-world/

Simply Needing More Money in Retirement

Living longer in retirement means needing more money. Period. Barring a huge lottery win or some crazy stock market action, the date you retire is likely the point at which you have the most money you will ever have. Not to put too grim a spin on it, but the problem with longevity is the further you get away from that date, the further your dollars have to stretch. If you only planned to live to a nice eighty-something but instead live to a nice 100-something, that is *two decades* you will need to account for monetarily.

To put this in perspective, let's say you like to drink coffee as an everyday splurge. Not accounting for inflation or leap years, a $4 cup-a-day habit is $29,200 over a two-decade span. Now, think of all the things you like to do that cost money. Add those up for twenty years of unanticipated costs. I think you'll see what I mean.

More Health Care Needs

In addition to the cost of living for a longer lifespan is the fact that aging — plain and simple — means more health care, and more health care means more money. Women are survivors. They suffer from the morbidity-mortality paradox, which states women suffer more non-fatal illnesses throughout their lifetime than men, who experience fewer illnesses but higher mortality.

Women have been found to seek treatment more often when not feeling well and emphasize staying healthy when older, according to studies. Survival, I believe, is on the side of the woman. However, surviving things (such as cancer) also means more checkups later in life.

A statistical concern for women involves the prospect of long-term care. Long-term care for women lasts 3.7 years on average compared to 2.2 years for men.[72]

Widowhood

Not only do women typically live longer than their same-age male counterparts, but they also stand a greater chance of living alone as they age. Some divorce, separate, or never marry. Among those age sixty-five and over, 33 percent of women live alone compared to 20 percent of men.[73]

I don't write this to scare people; rather, I think it's fundamentally important to prepare my female clients for something that may be a startling *but very likely* scenario. At some point, most women will have to handle their financial situations on their own. A little preparation can go a long way, and having a basic understanding of your household finances and the "who, what, where, and how much" of your family's assets is incredibly useful. It can prevent a tragic situation from being more traumatic.

In my opinion, the financial services industry sometimes underserves women in these situations. Some financial professionals tend to alienate women, even when their spouses are alive. I've heard several stories of women who sat through meeting after meeting without their financial professional ever addressing a single question to them.

In our firm, when we work with couples, we work hard to make sure our retirement income strategies work for *both* people. No matter who the financial alpha is, it's important for everyone affected by a retirement strategy to understand it.

---

[72] Lindsay Modglin. singlecare.com. February 15, 2022. "Long-term care statistics 2022" https://www.singlecare.com/blog/news/long-term-care-statistics/

[73] statistica.com. November 23, 2022. "Share of senior households living alone in the United States 2020, by gender" https://www.statista.com/statistics/912400/senior-households-living-alone-usa/

We also work hard to ensure that if our female clients become widows, we give them the time they need to grieve before getting into the nitty gritty of their new financial status. When we finally have that meeting, our goal is to help them navigate this new path on which they've suddenly found themselves. We help change Social Security benefits and ensure all their assets are still in place the way they should be. If their spouse had life insurance, we help them through the beneficiary process. Essentially, we help with everything we possibly can.

It's not uncommon for our firm to be the first phone call for someone after their spouse passes away. They call us even before they call their children or other family members because their finances are on top of their mind. Suddenly they're asking themselves, "What do I do?" Our job is to be there to provide answers and a guiding hand every step of the way.

Taxes

One of the often-unexpected aspects of widowhood is the tax bill. Many women continue similar lifestyles to the ones they shared with their spouses. This, in turn, means continuing to have a similar need for income. However, after the death of a spouse, their taxes will be calculated based on a single filer's income table, which is much less forgiving than the couple's tax rates. With proper planning, your financial professional and tax advisor may be able to help you take the sting out of your new tax status.

Caregiving

In addition to the financial burden created by caregiving responsibilities, many women often devote many hours each day to duties such as housekeeping and looking after loved ones. So then, when can women find the time to focus long and hard on financial matters?

Unfortunately, the impact and hardships created by traditional roles for women typically do not account for Social

Security benefit losses or the losses of health care benefits and retirement savings. This also doesn't account for maternity care, mothers who homeschool, or women who leave the workforce to care for their children in any way.

I don't repeat these statistics to scare you. In America, about 53 million serve as unpaid caregivers and spend roughly $7,000 annually on out-of-pocket caregiving costs.[74] Yet, I think the emotional value of the care many women provide their elderly relatives or neighbors cannot be quantified. So, to be clear, this shouldn't be taken as a "why not to provide caregiving" spiel. Instead, it should be seen as a call for "why to *prepare* for caregiving" or "how to lessen the financial and emotional burden of caregiving."

Funding Your Own Retirement

For these reasons, women should be prepared to fund more of their own retirements. There are several savings options and products, including the spousal IRA. They are like a typical IRA except used by a person who's married. The working spouse must earn at least as much money as is contributed into the IRA.[75] This is something to consider, particularly for families where one spouse has dropped out of the workforce to care for a relative. Also, if you find yourself in a caregiving role, talk to your employer's human resources department. Some companies have paid leave, special circumstances, or sick leave options you could qualify for, making it easier to cope and helping you stay longer in the workforce.

---

[74] TheScanFoundation.org. November 10, 2022. "Family caregivers are unsung heroes" https://www.thescanfoundation.org/the-buzz/family-caregivers-are-unsung-heroes.
[75] Andrea Coombes. Nerdwallet.com. November 2, 2023. "Spousal IRA: What It Is, How to Open One" https://www.nerdwallet.com/article/investing/spousal-ira-what-it-is-and-why-you-should-open-one

Saving Money

Women likely need more money to fund their retirements. But this doesn't have to be a significant burden. Often, women are better at saving, while usually taking less risk in their portfolios. One source identified many ways for how women are crushing this retirement component.[76]

- In a 2021 analysis of five million Fidelity customers over a ten-year period, women's investment rates of return outperformed men by .04 percent.
- Wells Fargo found that women take approximately 82 percent of the risk men take.
- Meghan Railey, co-founder and CEO of Optas Capital wrote, "While we have found that male clients tend to eagerly invest in the latest asset class everyone is talking about, like cryptocurrency, female clients do not generally jump on the shiny bandwagon."
- Women do a better job buying and holding quality stocks and avoid impulsive decisions. Staying invested for the long haul is often cited as the most effective investing strategy.
- Women remain calm and are less likely to liquidate their retirement accounts during market volatility.
- Lastly, Vanguard found women are less active investors, logging on to their accounts half as often as men and trading 40 percent less frequently.

With all the hurdles to retirement that are unique to women, it's exciting they inherently have an advantage when it comes to saving. This gives me reason to believe as women get more involved in their finances, families will continue to become more confident about retirement.

---

[76] Lyle Daly. The Motley Fool. September 26, 2023. "Investing for Women: What You Should Know"
https://www.fool.com/research/women-in-investing-research/

CHAPTER 10

Indexed Universal Life Insurance

My clients are not typically gamblers. A day at the poker table is more likely to give them nightmares than it is to make them eager with dollar signs in their eyes. Many would rather work with at least some guarantees than primarily with stocks and risk-based products, so of course, that often means turning more toward life insurance, and often to a product called indexed universal life insurance — also commonly referred to as fixed indexed universal life insurance.

If you've never heard of that before, I'm not surprised. This life insurance product isn't appropriate for everyone, but I want to take a second to talk about it because, for the right person, it can be a significant product in their financial arsenal.

Insurance: The Basics

If you haven't been casting around in the life insurance pond much, then let's take a second to cover the basics. During our working lives, it's likely we have some kind of basic term life policy, either privately or through our employers. Term life insurance means an individual is protected for a certain period of time — usually ten to thirty years. It typically correlates to a certain amount of wages (if it's an employer's plan) or a coverage amount chosen by the individual (if it's a person's private insurance).

At its most basic, term insurance provides funds for our loved ones and can be used for a number of purposes, including covering funeral expenses or something of that nature. Oftentimes, people will take out more than this. For instance, families with a stay-at-home parent sometimes purchase policies based on the working parent's life to cover years of income, plus the mortgage, etc. Your premium for a term life policy will be based on things like your coverage limit, your age, your health, and the term of the policy.

The older you are, the more likely it is you have health events or other issues that could make it more difficult to obtain term life insurance and the more expensive it is. Some consumers may see this as a disadvantage of term life insurance because they pay into a policy for twenty years. Then, it reaches its "endowment" — the end of the contract term — and there are no additional benefits.

Permanent Insurance

Aside from the basic term life policies many wage-earners hold, insurance companies also have permanent policies, also sometimes referred to as "cash value insurance." With a permanent insurance contract, your policy will typically remain in force as long as you continue to keep it funded (there is an exception for whole life policies, which we'll get to later). A permanent insurance contract has two pieces: the death benefit and cash value accumulation.

Both are spelled out in your contract. As these products gained recognition, people began to realize the products had significant advantages when it came to taxes. I don't want to get too technical, but it really is the technical details that make these policies valuable to their owners. That bit about tax advantages makes permanent life insurance policies attractive to consumers. Not only do they receive an income-tax-free death benefit for their beneficiaries, but they may also be able to borrow against their policy, income-tax-free, if they end up needing the money.

For example, let's say Eileen purchases a life insurance policy when she's thirty. She hates the idea of not having anything to show for her premiums over ten to twenty years, so she decides to use a permanent policy. Then, when she's close to fifty, her brother finds himself in dire straits. Eileen wants to help, and she's been a diligent saver. The catch is most of her money is in products like her 401(k) or an annuity. These may be products appropriate for her needs, but her circumstances have just changed, and she's looking for ways to help her sibling without incurring significant tax penalties.

But wait ... she has that permanent life insurance policy! She can borrow any accumulated cash value against her policy, free of income taxes. So, let's say she borrows a few thousand dollars from her policy. She doesn't have to pay taxes on any of it. She can pay it back into her policy at any time. Then, let's say Eileen dies before she "settles up" her policy (or pays back that loan). As long as she continues to pay premium payments or otherwise keeps her policy adequately funded until she dies, then her beneficiaries will still receive a death benefit minus the policy loan.

Are you with me so far? Here are the central themes on properly structured permanent life insurance policies: tax-free death benefit and income-tax-free withdrawals through policy loans are available as long as the premiums continue to be paid, and a minimum rate of cash value accumulation is guaranteed by the strength of the insurer.

Now, let's dive a little deeper into the two basic categories of permanent insurance on the market: whole life policies and universal life policies.

Whole Life Insurance

With whole life, an actuary in a back office has calculated what a person your age with your intended death benefit coverage, your health history, your potential lifespan — and other minutia — should pay for a premium rate. Depending on how the insurer calculates rate tables, your whole life policy will "endow" at a certain age — ninety, 100, 120, etc. — so there is the risk you could outlive the policy. The death benefit would pay out to you instead of your beneficiaries, which may create unplanned tax consequences.

Nonetheless, to qualify for your whole life policy, you will complete a medical questionnaire and possibly a paramedical exam, and based on that information, an underwriter will place you in one of these actuarial categories to determine your premium rate. One benefit of whole life insurance is the insurance company will credit a certain amount back into the policy's cash value based on your contract's guaranteed rate. Some insurance companies may also pay a dividend back to policyholders at the company's discretion.

Take Eileen from the preceding example, and let's consider the scenario if her permanent insurance policy was a whole life policy. When she first purchased the contract, the insurance agent would have been able to tell her what her locked-in premium rate would be. She would pay the same amount, year after year, to keep her contract in force. And she could also calculate her policy's minimum cash value to the penny.

Universal Life Insurance

If whole life is the basic permanent life insurance policy, universal is the souped-up model. It has eight speeds, comes in many colors, and has more options, which means it might take some extra time and research to be thoroughly understood. But this means if it's right for you, it can be even more customizable and fine-tuned to your specific needs.

The major differences:
- Flexible premium
- Increasing policy costs

Let's start with those increasing policy costs. Basically, the internal cost to the insurance company of maintaining your policy will increase over time, like a term insurance policy. Remember how whole life policies have those actuaries at the insurer's office calculating all of that and then determining a set rate for you to pay to cover it all? Well, with universal life, that's part of the flexible premium part. You can decide to pay a premium that will cover your future policy expenses, or you can decide to pay a premium that barely covers your current policy expenses, depending on your circumstances.

That is where these policies have gotten a bad rap in the past. If you purchase a policy and only ever pay the minimum premium required, your policy could lose value to the point that your premium no longer covers your policy's expenses, and then the policy would lapse. That's also why it's incredibly important to work with a financial professional you trust. This financial professional should shoot straight about whether this kind of product would be appropriate for you and make sure you fully understand all the details.

To return to our example of Eileen, though, here's how a well-set-up universal life insurance policy could work: Eileen, ever the diligent saver, would have paid well over the minimum premium every month. Every time she got a raise or payroll increase, she increased the amount of premium she paid into her policy. With the policy's contractual rate of interest, she had a substantial amount of cash value accumulated in the policy. That way, when she decided to borrow money against the policy to help her brother, she could even afford to decrease her monthly payments for a time, until she was back in a better financial position.

Indexing

Now to the main event: *indexed* universal life insurance (IUL). Like any permanent insurance, an IUL policy will remain in force as long as you continue to pay sufficient premiums, and you can borrow against your policy's cash value, income-tax-free. At their core, IUL policies are universal life insurance policies with flexible premiums. So, how are they different?

If you skim back through some of the other policy details, I covered the ability to withdraw the cash value of your policy without paying income taxes, even on the accumulation. Because of the index part of IULs, that accumulating cash value has the potential to accumulate more. An index is a tool that measures the movement of the market, like the S&P 500® or the Dow Jones Industrial Average. You can't invest directly in an index. It's just a sort of ruler.

With an IUL policy, your cash accumulation interest credits are based on an index, with what is called a "floor" and a "cap" or other limits such as a spread or participation rate. If the market does well, each year your policy can be credited interest on the cash accumulation based on whatever your policy's index is, subject to the cap, spread, or participation rate. If the market has a bad year and the index shows negative gains, your account still gets credited, whatever your contract floor is.

So, for example, let's say your contract cap is 12.5 percent and the floor is 0 percent. If the market returns 20 percent, your contract value gets a 12.5 percent interest credit. The next year, the S&P 500® returns a negative 26 percent. The insurance company won't credit your policy anything, but you also won't see your policy value slip because of that negative performance (although policy charges and expenses will still be deducted from your policy). So, your policy won't lose value because of poor market conditions, but you can still stand to realize interest credits due to changes in an index.

Another opportunity IUL policies present is for a policyholder to overfund the policy cash value in the first five or ten years and then, potentially, not have to pay any more money into the policy, letting the cash accumulation self-fund the policy. However, when overfunding an IUL policy, it is important to understand the policy may become a modified endowment contract (or MEC) if premium payments exceed certain amounts specified under the Internal Revenue Code.

This can happen if a policy has been funded too quickly in its early years. For MECs, distributions during the life of the insured (including loans) are fully taxable as income to the extent there is a gain in the policy over the amount of net premiums paid. An additional 10 percent federal income tax may apply for withdrawals made before age fifty-nine-and-one-half.

So, back to our friend, Eileen. If her permanent life insurance policy was an IUL, what might that have looked like? Eileen saves, paying well over the mandatory minimum of her IUL policy. Let's assume the market does well for decades. Her policy accumulates a significant cash value. At some point, she stops paying as much in premium, or maybe she stops paying any premium from her own pocket at all because her policy has enough cash value to pay for its own expenses with the insurance company. Then, when her brother needs help, there is enough cash value stored in the policy.

It's important to note that making withdrawals or taking policy loans from a policy may have an adverse effect. You may want to talk to your financial professional to re-evaluate your premium payment schedule if you are considering this option.

If you're reeling just a bit, it's understandable. There's a lot going on with these policies. If you don't take the time to understand the basics of how they work, it's entirely possible to fall behind on premium payments and end up with a policy that lapses. Yet, if you understand the terms of your contract and are working with purpose, IUL policies could be a powerful cog in the greater mechanics of your overall retirement strategy.

Just like annuities, IUL policies are a tool, and there are times when they are appropriate and times when they aren't. Typically, people use life insurance for two reasons: because they have a lot of money and want to mitigate their tax bill, or because they don't have enough money and their spouse won't be okay if they pass away. Ultimately, you must be sure IUL policies are the right tool for your unique situation.

Theoretically, you can pay a significant amount of premium into an IUL policy if you opt for a higher death benefit. I've never had someone pass away and hear anyone say, "Gosh, they had too much life insurance." In the event of premature death, this can be a great safeguard. For example, my wife's grandma is ninety-five, and her husband passed away over twenty years ago. Over that amount of time, her expenses have naturally gotten tighter and tighter. Having an IUL policy with a higher death benefit on her husband would have made those years a little easier, financially speaking.

Life happens. If you're married, and your spouse passes away early in retirement, the rules of the game change. The death benefit and the tax-free use of the IUL policy outside of the death benefit could both be great in this scenario. Again, it comes back to ensuring you use the right tool for the job. I don't use IULs every day for every client. Still, when it makes sense for a particular client and their situation, they can be a powerful component of an overall financial strategy.

CHAPTER 11

Finding a Financial Professional

I like to think of retirement as a 1,500-week vacation. To properly enjoy that vacation, you have to know if you can afford it, right? Even though my family didn't have much money while I was growing up, we still took a week-long vacation almost every year. Again, my parents weren't the greatest with money or budgeting, so there would be times when we weren't sure if we could afford to eat every day. If they had planned, saved, and had a budget they knew they could stick to, those vacations may have been a lot different.

The same rule applies for retirement. Having a plan helps ease the stress and allows you to fully enjoy that 1,500-week vacation. Not having a plan might mean it may not work out. Most people I know don't want to enter retirement just hoping that *maybe* it will work out. As much as we love the smell of French fries and the ambiance of McDonald's, most of us don't want to work there when we should be enjoying the next phase of our lives.

The last time I took a big vacation with my family, we wanted to go to Fiji and explore the different islands. As my wife and I tried to plan the details, she asked how we would get from one island to another. Swimming across thirty-eight miles of ocean didn't really appeal to either of us, nor did it seem the most practical solution. In the end, we hired a travel agent, which turned out to be a much better solution than trying to figure it all out on our own. We were able to rely on their experience and knowledge. We didn't have to worry about our budget because those details were worked out beforehand. In the end, we were able to focus on relaxing and enjoying our time together as a family.

When it comes to your 1,500-week vacation (retirement), the same logic applies. Just as our travel agent used their industry knowledge and years of experience to help us plan our dream vacation, an experienced financial planner can help you plan your dream retirement—because that's what they do every day.

When it comes to finding the right financial planner, there are some key factors to keep in mind. For starters, you want to hire a professional who focuses on retirement planning. Some financial professionals only focus on growing your money. That might be fine when you're twenty-two, but as you prepare for retirement, you need someone who focuses on making sure the money you have saved doesn't run out before you need it to. Retirement planning is an entirely different skill set.

Think of it like this. If you had a heart problem, you wouldn't go to your family's general practitioner for care, right? You would go to a specialist. A lot of times, you might even see three or four before deciding which treatment to follow. It's the same with retirement planning. I always encourage people to interview several retirement planners before deciding who to work with. Doing so also helps ensure you find someone you like and trust. This is paramount, especially if you are married. Ask yourself, "If I'm not here, do I trust this person will have my wife or husband's priorities at heart?" Trust is the most important aspect of any relationship.

Of course, there are plenty of reasons to disqualify a potential financial advisor, and I would argue the biggest is if you simply don't like the person for whatever reason. If you don't feel completely comfortable with them or are unsure if you should trust everything they're telling you, that's a valid reason to forego working with them. Do your homework, research the advisor as best you can, and ask a lot of questions.

A good retirement planner will welcome clients who take an active interest in the planning process. Remember, when you decide to work with a retirement planner, your relationship will likely last many years. That's why it's so important to choose someone you're entirely comfortable with, trust, and who will be honest with you—even if the news isn't what you want to hear.

Let's revisit my parents' situation. Remember, I had told my dad his only option (at that time) was to plan on retiring late or dying early. He was understandably upset. After that conversation, my dad—a life-long smoker—developed diverticulitis and spent three days in the hospital. When he came out, he quit smoking. He'd quit for three days while in the hospital and saw no reason he couldn't do it forever. That was a big change.

The next big change my parents made was to stop eating out as much. My mom is a great cook, so they started eating at home more. They got serious about money and changing bad habits for the first time. They put their heads to the ground and went from spending every dollar to saving twenty-five cents on every dollar they made. They made a lot of positive improvements that show just how effective change can be. I won't lie; it wasn't easy. It took a lot of dedicated effort, but they had a goal, and together they were able to develop a plan to help them achieve it.

As I've mentioned, my parents are a great success story. They were able to retire at ages sixty-two and sixty-four. They live in a cottage on the lake and have a pontoon boat. They're not living an extravagant, jet-setting lifestyle by any means, but they're happy and a long way from living paycheck-to-Wednesday. Ultimately, they accomplished what they did by taking small, consistent steps and following their specific plan. In this way, they were able to scale the financial mountain.

Remember the C.L.I.M.B. process (Conserve and Grow Assets, Lifetime Income, Insure Your Health, Minimize Taxes, and Build a Legacy). For every plan, I help my clients design accounts for each of these elements, but everyone climbs the retirement mountain in their own way. Your C.L.I.M.B. might involve adjusting your investments to better align with your unique goals and risk tolerance. Maybe you need to make adjustments for tax purposes. Whatever your situation, your financial planner should be there to help guide you up the mountain to the summit (retirement). At Jones Retirement Advisors, that's exactly what we do for our clients. We're with you every step of the way.

    Let's get climbing.

Acknowledgments

I would like to express my deepest gratitude to the incredible individuals who have made an indelible impact on my life, my career, and my journey in writing this book.

First and foremost, I want to thank my loving wife, Angela, whose unwavering support and belief in me has been invaluable. Thank you for always being my rock.

To my amazing daughter, Eleanor: watching you grow and thrive has been a constant source of joy and inspiration. Thank you for reminding me why I do what I do.

To my incredible parents who gave me an incredible childhood and shaped me into the person I am today: thank you for your influence, your guidance, your patience, and your willingness to be such a big part of this book. Without you, this book would not exist.

I would also like to extend my heartfelt thanks to my clients for their continued trust and support, and to everyone who reads this book. Thank you for joining me on this journey and for allowing me to share my stories with you.

About the Author

BRAD JONES
Founder and Financial Advisor
Jones Retirement Advisors

As the founder of Jones Retirement Advisors, Brad is dedicated to helping clients create financial independence through a well-thought-out financial strategy for retirement.

As a junior in high school, Brad knew he wanted to be a financial advisor and help others work toward their retirement dreams. After high school, he attended Eastern Michigan University and graduated with his bachelor's degree in finance.

Following college, he spent the first decade of his career with a regional consulting firm honing his skills. He went on to open his own firm and focus on his love of providing retirement advice. With more than eighteen years of experience working with retirees and those near retirement, Brad enjoys connecting with clients and prospects by conducting informational seminars in the community.

Brad is a family-centered person. In November of 2021, Brad and his wife Angie welcomed their first child, Eleanor Grace. The family includes rescue dogs Lucy and Ocque. When he's not in the office, Brad enjoys golfing, taking the dogs to the park, and creating memories with his family.*

---

* Securities products and services made available through AE Financial Services, LLC (AEFS), member FINRA/SIPC. Investment advisory products and services made available through AE Wealth Management, LLC (AEWM), a Registered Investment Advisor. Insurance products are offered through the insurance business Jones Retirement Advisors, LLC. Jones Retirement Advisors, LLC is also a Financial Services practice that offers products and services through AE Financial Services, LLC (AEFS), member FINRA/SIPC. Jones Retirement Advisors, LLC is also an Investment Advisory practice that offers investment advisory products and services through AE Wealth Management, LLC (AEWM), a Registered Investment Advisor. AEFS and AEWM do not offer insurance products. The insurance products offered by Jones Retirement Advisors, LLC are not subject to regulatory requirements or standards of care applicable to registered representatives and are not subject to Investment Advisor requirements. AEFS, AEWM & Jones Retirement Advisors, LLC are not affiliated companies.

www.ingramcontent.com/pod-product-compliance
Lightning Source LLC
Chambersburg PA
CBHW052210220526
45471CB00004B/1901